Graham Scholes

Thorneywood,
Nottingham
17 February 2006
(navigator on "Handley Page
Halifax" bombers, 1943, with
158 Squadron, Royal Air Force.
Lissett, East Yorkshire.
Aged 21.

26, Florence Road,
as above. This superb
book from "Military &
Aviation Book Society."

Graham saw the Lancaster, NX611,
"Just Jane" when it taxied at
East Kirkby, Lincs. on 12th. July 06.

LIVING
LANCASTERS

**To joyride in a Lancaster is sheer pleasure.
To carry out a bombing operation is sheer terror.**

Anonymous member of Bomber Command Lancaster Aircrew

LIVING LANCASTERS

KEEPING THE LEGEND ALIVE

Jarrod Cotter

SUTTON PUBLISHING

IN ASSOCIATION WITH

First published in the United Kingdom in 2005 by
Sutton Publishing Limited · Phoenix Mill
Thrupp · Stroud · Gloucestershire · GL5 2BU

In association with *Flypast Magazine*.

British Library Cataloguing in Publication Data
A catalogue record for this book is available from the British Library.

ISBN 0-7509-4192-8

Typeset in 10/14 pt Sabon.
Typesetting and origination by
Sutton Publishing Limited.
Printed and bound in England by
J.H. Haynes & Co. Ltd, Sparkford.

Dedication

To my loving wife Clare and my two wonderful sons Jamie and Matthew. The boys have both developed their own interest in Lancasters, which has afforded me the tremendous opportunity to share my passion and work with them as they've grown up. And sorry, Clare, for all those weeks and weekends away!

To my Mum and Dad, Margaret and George Cotter, who have supported and encouraged my fascination with historic aircraft since it began – including everything from buying me model kits to spend hours building and painting them, to taking me to Hendon, where I gazed respectfully at S-Sugar as I got my first close-up sight of a real Lancaster.

No book of this nature could be written without paying a special tribute to the more than 55,000 Bomber Command aircrew – each one somebody's son, father, husband or brother – who didn't come home. Their memories live on whenever four Merlins burst into life. . . .

My sons Jamie (right) and Matthew at East Kirkby after seeing a taxiing demonstration by NX611 *Just Jane*.

Night falls as PA474 sits outside its hangar, the reflection of which is visible on the glass of the bomb aimer's position. *(Keith Brenchley)*

Contents

OC BBMF Sqn Ldr Clive Rowley MBE was of great assistance with various aspects of this book, especially the supply of photographs and with directing me towards the right department to obtain a Crown Copyright licence for their publication. As a fighter pilot, Clive is appropriately seen with Spitfire IX MK356 as a backdrop.

Acknowledgements

As is always the case with a project of this kind, to name everyone who helped in the preparation of this book just isn't possible, I'm afraid. But I would like to pay particular thanks to the following, who were instrumental in making it possible in so many ways.

Battle of Britain Memorial Flight
Flt Lt Ed Straw for his continuous generous help and cooperation – it was Ed's trust in me to report on the BBMF responsibly that made it possible for me to be able to consider writing a book like this. OC BBMF Sqn Ldr Clive Rowley MBE, former OC BBMF Sqn Ldr Paul Day OBE, AFC, BBMF 'Bomber Leader' Sqn Ldr Stu Reid, Wg Cdr Paul Willis, Sqn Ldr Andy Marson, Sqn Ldr Jeff Hesketh, Flt Lt Garry Simm, Flt Lt Jack Hawkins, C/T Keith Brenchley, C/T Paul Blackah and J/T Chris Elcock.

Lincolnshire Aviation Heritage Centre
Fred Panton MBE, Harold Panton, Sqn Ldr Ken 'Jacko' Jackson MBE, AFC, Flt Lt Mike Chatterton, Ian Hickling, Robert Gibson-Bevan and Mark Fletcher.

Canadian Warplane Heritage Museum
Chairman of the Board R.J. Franks, Don Schofield, Don Fisher, Lancaster Crew Chiefs Jeff Young and Randy Straughan, Chief Engineer Duane Freeman, Marketing Manager Robin Hill and Curator Chad Martin.

Australian War Memorial
Former Head of Media Ian Kelly and Media Assistant Laura Ryan.

Royal Air Force Museum London
Public Relations Manager Ajay Srivastava, Aircraft Technician John O'Neill and Department of Aircraft and Exhibits Curator Andy Simpson.

Thanks to Tracey Woods, Marketing and PR Manager at IWM Duxford, Mervyn Hallam at RAF Scampton, Sqn Ldr Dick James at IX(B) Sqn, RAF Marham, Kenny and Lisa Love at the Temora Aviation Museum, Martin Collins, Pete Day, Brian Goulding and Wouter van Warmelo for their assistance with either locating or supplying some of the historic pictures.

My appreciation also goes to the publishers and authors of four great books that concentrate on the principal Lancasters featured here, for giving me permission to use their works as sources of reference for the histories and restorations of the relevant aircraft. They are: Lex McAulay, publisher, Banner Books, *G-for-George*; Ray Leach, author, *A Lancaster at Peace*; Brian Goulding, co-author, *Story of a Lanc*; plus John Denison, publisher, The Boston Mills Press, and Bette Page, author, *Mynarski's Lanc*. And thanks go to Andy Simpson at the RAF Museum for providing me with a detailed history of R5868 *S-Sugar*.

Thanks are also due to Adrian Cox and Ken Ellis at Key Publishing Ltd, for allowing me access to a great amount of company material that I used; also to Ken for advice and proof-reading, and to my colleague and friend on *FlyPast*, Assistant Editor Nigel Price, for help with survivors, museums and website information.

Much appreciation goes to Key Publishing's Chief Photographer Duncan Cubitt, not only for putting his back out during air-to-air photographic sorties, but also for the countless hours he spent patiently working on digital pictures, and finally for letting me take him back around the Australian War Memorial for one more look at 'Striking by Night' on a 'day off' when I should have been offering to take him to the bar!

And thanks also to Jonathan Falconer at Sutton Publishing, for agreeing to publish this book when I offered it and for his help, advice, and patience with my foibles ever since.

But I must finish by thanking David Brown at Warners Group Publications plc in Bourne, Lincolnshire. David was the first in the publishing world to believe in me and he gave me my break. Without him I would never have had such firm foundations in this field and the opportunity to get this far. Thanks Browny!

All photography is by the author unless otherwise stated.

Flt Lt Ed Straw at the controls of BBMF's Lancaster PA474.
(Rachel Warnes)

Foreword

I feel very privileged being entrusted to fly the Battle of Britain Memorial Flight (BBMF) Lancaster. For me, like the rest of the crew, it is a great honour.

I was first drawn to the magic of the aircraft when as a small boy I watched the film *The Dam Busters* with my Dad. The fascination grew through models, posters and books, and I soon became a regular at air shows, experiencing the unique sights and sounds of the Lancaster. I remember well my first visit to the BBMF hangar at RAF Coningsby and the unforgettable thrill of seeing this magnificent aeroplane at such close quarters. My mind was made up: if I succeeded in becoming an RAF pilot, I wanted to fly the Lancaster. I joined the RAF in 1986, and sixteen years later that dream came true.

The BBMF Lancaster is not modernised in any way. It is a wonderful aircraft and flies just as Roy Chadwick intended. However, like many, I can only guess what it must have been like for the crews of Bomber Command to operate the aircraft throughout the sustained bomber offensive of the Second World War. When we marvel at the Lancaster in flight today, it is easy to forget the pivotal role it played in one of the most bitter and costly battles of the war. The Germans had developed a fearsome defensive system that was the best in the world. By the end of the war, their night-fighters and flak batteries destroyed more than 8,000 Allied bombers – 3,345 of them Lancasters. Of the 125,000 men who volunteered to fly with Bomber Command, more than 55,000 lost their lives. Thousands more were injured or mentally broken by their ordeal. The statistics are truly horrific: the crews of Bomber Command sustained a loss rate never before borne by any military force of comparable size throughout history.

Author Jarrod Cotter has travelled worldwide to collate the most up-to-date record of active Lancasters. I know well his love of the aircraft and his enormous respect for the men who flew them operationally. Backed by an extensive library of pictures, his book provides a wonderful insight into today's 'living' Lancasters, as well as providing a flavour of the type's illustrious past. My hope is that this book will help launch new generations into the world of the Lancaster and that, so inspired, they will go on to discover more about the epic exploits of the men of Bomber Command during the Second World War. Keeping alive their bravery is our aim as bomber crew at the BBMF. We believe that, as long as the Lancaster continues to fly, the men of Bomber Command – particularly the 55,000 who gave their all for our freedom – will always be remembered.

Lest we forget.

Ed Straw, Lancaster captain,
Battle of Britain Memorial Flight

(Crown Copyright/MOD)

With a bright moon shining above it on a clear night, NX611 superbly re-creates the atmosphere of Lancaster night operations at East Kirkby, Lincolnshire.

Introduction

Of the 7,377 Avro Lancasters that were built, it's startling to realise that only seventeen remain as more or less complete airframes around the world. It is no wonder then that those which do survive are so highly cherished, in most cases maintained in pristine condition so as to pay tribute to the many brave crews who fought in them. Go to any air show or museum where a Lancaster is on display, whether flying or static, and it will always steal the show. This popularity proves that the Lancaster's iconic status has waned little since the Second World War when it played a principal role in maintaining the freedom of our country.

My own fascination with the 'Lanc' goes back as far as I can remember. Therefore, during the course of my work as Deputy Editor on *FlyPast* Magazine, the UK's top-selling aviation monthly, it is always a particular pleasure when I go out to cover a story about a Lancaster.

As I began to get to know better those who maintain these aircraft, I also began to realise what fascinating background information lies behind the finished product. Of course, for the most part that finished product is all we see, and as we gaze in awe perhaps we take it for granted that the propellers turn, and that the aircraft has arrived on time, displayed to us in a manner that shows off the type to its best advantage. But to get one of the airworthy Lancasters to a venue on time when, for example, the weather is nearing

the limits or there has been a recent 'snag', calls for a great deal of behind-the-scenes work that often goes well above and beyond the call of duty. After witnessing this first-hand, I have been filled with admiration that this kind of dedication is commonplace within the world of Lancaster preservation. Aircrews, ground crews, museum staff and volunteers – they all invest their time without hesitation to make sure that their aircraft pay a special tribute to the British and Commonwealth bomber crews of the Second World War.

As well as rightly honouring the surviving veterans who attend the many and various events, whenever the sound of the bomber roars overhead a particularly emotive 'living' tribute goes out to the more than 55,000 Bomber Command aircrew who never made it home. And that's what made this book particularly moving for me to write. I have been extremely fortunate to be on board a Lancaster on a number of occasions as the four Merlins have burst into life. Obviously, this has always been an absolute pleasure, and something exciting to tell my family when I arrived home.

However, had this been 1943 it would have been an entirely different matter. Knowing what I do today, I'm sure that as the engines fired up I would have been filled with apprehension about whether or not I would make it home to see my loved ones again. This point is brought home by

Looking out at Toronto from Canadian Warplane Heritage Museum's Lancaster Mk.X, FM213. Toronto is located on the northern shore of Lake Ontario, and noticeable to the left of the CN Tower is the city's Island Airport.

Wg Cdr Guy Gibson VC, DSO*, DFC*, in some words from the Foreword and Dedication of his famous book *Enemy Coast Ahead*: 'One moment they are together living their own lives and happy; a man and wife walking hand in hand down a country lane may be separated, perhaps for ever . . .

'Picture peaceful England on a cool spring evening; the flowers are blooming, the hum of serenity is in the air. Suddenly there is a snarl of four motors, and a few hours later your airman is fighting the hell of flak and destruction over the target.

'At home they wait, brave and patient, asking the same questions again and again: I hope he gets back all right; when are they due?'

I also vividly remember talking to a former member of Bomber Command Lancaster aircrew who had completed a tour of operations during the Second World War. He said to me that one of his crewmates once commented: 'To joyride in a Lancaster is sheer pleasure. To carry out a bombing operation is sheer terror.'

It has only been possible for me to write this book because of the generosity shown to me by so many of those associated with the remaining Lancasters. It is the culmination of several years work during which I was afforded incredible access, both on the ground and in the air.

As I lifted off from Hamilton International Airport on board FM213 en route for Toronto, I was overwhelmed that along the way I had become one of very few people to have flown in both the world's airworthy Lancasters. I was so inspired flying around the CN Tower that it confirmed to me that what I have seen and experienced through the courtesy of the owners and operators of these wonderful aircraft could form the basis of a book in which I could share with a large audience the stories of these Living Lancasters.

In this volume I have combined historical overviews of the principally featured aircraft with material from various articles I have written on surviving Lancs, then added new information to present the complete story in this book. Many of the pictures are previously unpublished and much of what is shown in them is rarely seen.

If I have achieved the aim I had in mind, the next time you see a Lancaster at an air show or museum I hope that you will have gained a little more insight into everything that's gone into its appearance there, and thus you will ultimately enjoy and appreciate it all the more.

Jarrod Cotter, Lincolnshire,
October 2005

Wg Cdr Guy Gibson VC, DSO*, DFC*, leader of the legendary 617 Sqn on the 'Dam Busters' raid. *(Courtesy RAF Scampton Historical Museum)*

CHAPTER 1
Birth of a Legend

The Avro Lancaster was the most famous and successful heavy bomber flown by the Royal Air Force during the Second World War. It is a legend that lives on to this day, its contribution to maintaining the freedom of our nation never likely to be forgotten.

A.V. Roe & Company Ltd first flew the Avro 679 Manchester twin-engined medium bomber on 25 July 1939 from Ringway, Manchester. The Manchester was the brainchild of Avro's Chief Designer, Roy Chadwick, and was powered by a pair of Rolls-Royce Vulture engines. By the end of January 1940, some 1,200 Manchesters had been ordered, but only 200 were delivered due to reliability problems with the Vulture. With the Rolls-Royce Merlin proving to be an excellent engine, and with more powerful marks in the planning, it was decided not to waste any time in trying to improve the Vulture. This cancellation left Avro with a superb airframe just needing a reliable powerplant.

In February 1940 discussions had taken place regarding a proposed Manchester III powered by four Merlins. There was some initial reluctance about this, as at the time Merlins were desperately needed for Hawker Hurricanes and Supermarine Spitfires. However, in July 1940 there was a change of heart and the Air Ministry informed Avro of its wish that the development of the four-engined Manchester should go ahead.

The Avro 683 was to differ only slightly from the production Manchester, which had already received approval for an increase of its wingspan from 80ft to 90ft. The new design had a proposed wingspan of 100ft (the Lancaster eventually featured a 102ft wingspan). To meet the demanding schedules, it was strongly felt that retention of the Avro 679 centre section would be crucial.

After a number of setbacks, Avro got the approval to produce two prototypes by July 1941. The first of these, BT308, was rolled out for engine runs on 28 December 1940. By 4 January 1941, the four-engined Avro 683 was cleared to fly from Woodford, Manchester. However, due to poor weather – low cloud, drizzle and fog – it was temporarily grounded.

By 9 January the weather had improved sufficiently for BT308 to take to the skies – and the legend was born. While the aircraft was still widely known as the Manchester III, it was annotated as a Lancaster on its Air Ministry Form 1187 'design certificate for flight trials'.

BT308 initially featured a triple-fin design. However, following early handling trials it was suggested that the aircraft be fitted with larger twin fins and the central fin be removed. It was first flown in this form on 21 February 1941, and such was the improvement that on its second test flight BT308 was flown with both port engines stopped, proving that the larger rudders could keep the bomber flying straight.

Lancaster prototype BT308 in its original triple-fin configuration, seen at Boscombe Down in January 1941. The aircraft visible in the background is a Blackburn Roc. *(Key Collection)*

The second prototype, DG595, carried out its maiden flight on 13 May 1941. It quickly received authorisation to go for service trials. This was met with delays, but Roy Chadwick used the time wisely and set about improving a number of areas he had already identified as needing attention, as well as initiating a complete review of the aircraft and its systems. With Manchester production now ceased, the Lancaster was approved and the balance of orders was changed to the new four-engined bomber. The first production machine, L7527, flew on 31 October 1941.

L7527 differed from the prototypes in that it had four 1,280hp Merlin XXs rather than the 1,145hp Merlin Xs. The aircraft's performance was simply outstanding; large-scale production soon began at several factories, and plans were also put in place to see the Lancaster built in

Canada (more details of the Canadian-built Lancaster Xs can be found in Chapter 3 on FM213 and at the Canadian Warplane Heritage Museum).

The first RAF unit to receive the Lanc, 44 (Rhodesia) Sqn, took delivery of three examples of the type at Waddington, Lincolnshire, on Christmas Eve 1941. However, it was not until 3 March 1942 that the Lancaster entered operational service, when four aircraft from 44 Sqn set off for Heligoland Bight off The Netherlands on a mine-laying sortie. The Lancasters set out from Waddington at 1815hrs and all returned safely around five hours later.

The first night-bombing op with Lancasters took place a week later on 10/11 March, when two 44 Sqn Lancs took part in a raid on Essen. Each of the Lancasters carried 5,000lb of incendiaries, and they joined a force of 126 bombers which included Handley Page Hampdens, Manchesters, Short Stirlings and Vickers Wellingtons. The Lancasters were certainly well received by their crews, and they quickly settled into squadron service, proving themselves to be sound and reliable workhorses.

Many raids by Lancasters would go on to make headline news, and the first of these was the daylight operation by 44 and 97 Sqns to bomb the MAN Diesel factory at Augsburg, Germany, on 17 April 1942. Sqn Ldr J.D. Nettleton VC of 44 Sqn led the twelve-aircraft op, for which he became the first of ten Lancaster aircrew to be awarded the Victoria Cross for their exploits in this aircraft.

Lancasters were in service in time to participate on the first 'Thousand Bomber Raid' on the night of 30/31 May 1942, codenamed

The crew of 9 Sqn's W4964 WS-J on night ops. This Lanc became famous after completing 106 operations wearing its 'Johnny Walker' nose art. W4964's 100th op occurred on the first attempt by 9 and 617 Sqns to bomb the *Tirpitz* on 15 September 1944. *(Courtesy IX Squadron Archives)*

Operation Millennium. Out of a total of 1,047 aircraft that were dispatched to Cologne, 868 reached the primary target.

On the clear moonlit night of 16/17 May 1943, the newly formed 617 Sqn successfully carried out what became the most famous single operation in the history of aerial warfare. The squadron, commanded by Wg Cdr Guy Gibson, set out from Scampton in Lincolnshire to breach key dams in the industrial heartland of Germany. For the sortie the squadron used a special weapon (codenamed 'Upkeep' and actually termed a mine, but more commonly referred to as the 'bouncing bomb'), which had been designed by the famous and highly respected aviation designer Barnes Wallis.

The Lancasters used for the raid were B.III (Specials) modified to be able to carry the weapon in a purpose-designed holding device which could rotate it at the necessary 500rpm it would need to work successfully. Furthermore, the bomb would need to be dropped from just 60ft, at night, and at a specified speed and an exact distance from the dams. To compound things further, the crews had just seven weeks to train for the precision attack, as it had to take place within a small window of opportunity.

Nineteen aircraft set out, with sixteen reaching the targets. Operation Chastise was carried out successfully, with the Möhne and Eder Dams both being breached and the Sorpe damaged. Eight Lancasters were lost and only three of their fifty-six crew members survived to become prisoners of war.

It was for this famous operation that Guy Gibson was awarded the Victoria Cross, and a total of thirty-four decorations were awarded to aircrew who participated on Chastise. The post-raid publicity was massive, and proved to be a tremendous PR boost for the RAF.

Another very famous achievement using Lancs came about as a result of the three operations mounted to sink the mighty German battleship *Tirpitz*. Along with 617 Sqn, as the war progressed 9 Sqn also specialised in dropping large bombs, in particular the 12,000lb Tallboy, on strategic targets, and the ops aimed at destroying the *Tirpitz* are a further good example of the operational versatility of the Lanc.

In January 1942 Prime Minister Winston Churchill put out a document to the Chiefs of Staff stating that no other sea target was comparable to the *Tirpitz* – the entire worldwide naval situation would be altered if it could be destroyed, or even crippled. Although a number of attempts by various units were made to sink the vessel, it remained serviceable. So the two squadrons, 9 and 617, were tasked to bomb the *Tirpitz* during September 1944 on Operation Paravane. Armed with Tallboys, they were to fly to Yagodnik in the Soviet Union so that they could be within range of the battleship.

A number of aircraft from both squadrons were lost en route to Yagodnik, but the remaining force of Lancasters set out from the Russian airfield on 15 September to bomb the *Tirpitz* in its Norwegian hiding place at Kåafjord. The crucial element of surprise was lost when a German ground unit gave prior notice of the bomber force's direction, and a smokescreen was set up over the ship. Attempts were made to bomb the *Tirpitz*, but many of the post-flight reports state that the target was obscured by smoke, making results difficult to determine.

Later it was discovered that the *Tirpitz* had been hit by a Tallboy that had gone through the forward deck and emerged below the waterline on the starboard side before exploding, and a second near miss had caused further damage. The bombs are thought to have been dropped by 9 Sqn's Flt Lt J.D. Melrose and 617's Wg Cdr J.B. Tait DSO*, DFC***. The attack had, however, rendered *Tirpitz* unfit to go to sea.

The damage was patched up by mid-October, and the huge vessel was moved to the port of

This superb painting by Philip E. West entitled *Primary Target* depicts Lancaster B.III (Special) ED906 AJ-J flown by Flt Lt D.J.H. Maltby DSO, DFC, which delivered the 'Upkeep' mine that breached the Möhne Dam on 17 May 1943. Several previous direct hits from other 617 Sqn aircraft didn't actually breach the substantial structure, which was designated Target 'X', and the code word for the release of one of the special weapons was 'Goner'. After David Maltby's bomb, the codeword 'Nigger' was sent out, signifying that the Möhne had been breached and the aircraft were to divert to Target 'Y', the Eder Dam. This painting was published as a limited edition print by SWA Fine Art Publishers of Bath in 2001, and in my opinion it remains just the most striking picture depicting the Dams raid that I have ever seen. *(Courtesy SWA Fine Art Publishers)*

Tromsø, around 200 miles south of its previous location. This new berth put the battleship within a potential range of RAF bases in north-east Scotland, including Lossiemouth.

In order to carry out these operations, the Lancasters would have to be heavily modified and fitted with the more powerful Merlin 24s – but the only ones available were already fitted to other Lancs scattered throughout 5 Gp. A frantic search located all the Merlin 24s, which were then exchanged with the engines fitted to the Tallboy aircraft, and in turn the lower-powered units were installed on the Main Force Lancasters.

Other modifications included removing the mid-upper turrets pilot's armour, guns and ammo from the front turrets and gas bottles, as well as reducing the amount of ammo carried in the rear turret. Extra fuel tanks were then fitted to give the aircraft sufficient range.

More than 120 engines were exchanged over a three-day period – this and all the other modifications had to be carried out on top of routine maintenance and repairs, thus confirming 9 Sqn's unofficial motto: 'There's always bloody something!'

A combined force of forty Lancasters (twenty from 9 Sqn, nineteen from 617 Sqn and PD329 from 463 Sqn on 'special photographic duties') left their bases for Scotland on 28 October, and the following day set off for Tromsø on Operation Obviate. Heavily laden with extra fuel and weighty Tallboys, the aircraft took off at +18 boost rather than the normal +14.

As the force approached the target area, an unexpected weather front caused conditions to deteriorate rapidly with bombing being made difficult as the target quickly became obscured by cloud. Some aircraft dropped bombs by targeting

12/11	LANCASTER FB.696	F/L.F.G.LAKE	Bombing "TIRPITZ"	0322	1548	Primary attacked 0937 hours. 16000 ft.
		SGT. R.W.BAIRD				Five bombs seen to fall. No. 1 - 50 yards off bow of
		F/O.J.A.PATERSON (CAN)				ship. No. 2 - slightly undershot centre of ship. No. 3 -
		W/O.G.R.WATTS (CAN)				about 30 yards from stern. No. 4- overshot centre of ship
		F/S.G.R.PARKINSON				by about 150 yards. No. 5- overshot to the right by about
		F/S.J.S.PARKS.				150 yards. In addition Rear Gunner saw own bomb which he
						considers hit the ship as a big explosion and fire
						followed immediately.
12/11	LANCASTER FB.368 A	S/L.A.G.WILLIAMS	Bombing. "TIRPITZ"	0328	1551	Primary attacked 0945 hours. 16000 ft.
		SGT.G.V.PRETTEJOHNS				Very near miss on starboard side aft seen just before
		F/O.R.C.HARVEY				bombing and about three other bombs seen to burst close
		F/S.A.H.HORRY				to the ship. One hit believed as a column of smoke
		SGT.P.A.MORGAN				enveloped the ship and its guns stopped firing.
		SGT.A.B.WATT.				
12/11	LANCASTER LM.220 Y	F/O.W.D.TWEDDLE	Bombing "TIRPITZ"	0316	1553	Primary attacked 0945½ hours. 14,600 ft.
		SGT.C.G.HEATH				On run up one bomb seen to hit fjord side of ship and
		F/O.E.SHIELDS.				only one gun on fjord side continued firing afterwards.
		F/O.D.A.NOLAN.				After leaving the target a large explosion was seen at
		F/S. A. CARSON.				0947 hours.
		SGT.K.MALLINSON.				
12/11	LANCASTER NF.939	F/O.A.E.JEFFS.	Bombing "TIRPITZ"	0327	1512	Primary attacked 0947 hours. 14200 ft.
		SGT.C.V.HIGGINS				Ship seen on run-up, but just before release of bomb
		SGT.K.C.MOUSLEY				smoke obscured target. Bomb was aimed at centre of smoke.
		SGT.H.A.FISHER				No hit seen, but bombs seen bursting all round ship.
		SGT.C.M.McMILLAN				
		SGT.G.J.SYMONDS				

A page from 9 Sqn Operations Record Book, showing sorties for 12 November 1944, when the *Tirpitz* was finally destroyed. The third entry down lists that of Fg Off Dougie Tweddle and his crew of LM220 'Y', which is claimed by 9 Sqn to have delivered the bomb that dealt the fatal blow to the mighty German battleship.
(Courtesy IX Squadron Archives)

the gun flashes they could glimpse through the cloud, but as the force turned home the crews knew the *Tirpitz* was still afloat. It was later reported that, had the attack happened just half an hour earlier, conditions would have been perfect.

A third attempt by 9 and 617 Sqns to bomb the *Tirpitz* was initiated during November. At 0300hrs on the morning of 12 November 1944, the first of the Lancasters set off from Scotland on Operation Catechism. On this day they had perfect weather conditions all the way to the target, with the clear sky offering excellent visibility.

As the Lancasters neared the battleship, they were greeted by flak. With their armament depleted to save weight, there was a more serious risk that the Lancasters could become very easy prey to the *Tirpitz*'s fighter cover. Indeed, ground troops reported the bomber force to be heading towards the vessel, and its captain ordered that the fighters be scrambled, knowing they could be overhead in ten minutes. However, the eighteen Focke-Wulf Fw 190s that got aloft set off in the wrong direction; they had apparently not been informed of the battleship's change of anchorage.

Everything was at last in favour of a successful attack; the Tallboys rained down on the *Tirpitz*, and after a number of direct hits and near misses the battleship rolled over to port and lay on its side. Huge clouds of black smoke rose up into the gin-clear sky above the *Tirpitz* – the crews' determination to finish off this significant threat had finally paid off.

One of the first bombs to hit the battleship is thought to have been dropped by Wg Cdr Tait of 617 Sqn. But 9 Sqn laid claim to sinking the *Tirpitz*, as following 617's bomb run it is reported that the ship's guns were still firing when 9 Sqn's aircraft began to attack. The belief at 9 Sqn is that Fg Off Dougie Tweddle and his crew of LM220 WS-Y delivered the bomb that

Ten Lancaster aircrew won Britain's highest award for gallantry, the Victoria Cross. In date order of the operations for which the medals were awarded, the recipients were: Sqn Ldr John Nettleton VC (17 April 1942); Wg Cdr Guy Gibson VC, DSO*, DFC* (16/17 May 1943); Flt Lt William Reid VC (3 December 1943); Sgt Norman Jackson VC (26 April 1944); Plt Off Andrew Mynarski VC (12 June 1944); Sqn Ldr Ian Bazalgette VC, DFC (4 August 1944); Wg Cdr Leonard Cheshire VC, DSO**, DFC (8 September 1944); Sqn Ldr Robert Palmer VC, DFC* (23 December 1944); Flt Sgt George Thompson VC (1 January 1945); and Capt Edwin Swales VC, DFC (23 February 1945).

completed the task. The debate between the two squadrons goes on to this day . . .

After the Tallboy came the 22,000lb Grand Slam bomb. To carry this the Lancaster had again to be modified, with the huge bombs being slung externally in a doorless bomb bay. The first use of the Grand Slam came on 14 March 1945, when the Bielefeld Viaduct was attacked. The

Lancasters capable of carrying Grand Slams became known as 'Clapper' aircraft by their crews, because after releasing their heavy payloads the aircraft 'went like the clappers'!

Another high-profile mission which came late in the war was the daylight raid to bomb Hitler's 'Eagle's Nest' retreat at Berchtesgaden. This op to the Bavarian Alps was carried out on 25 April

Night operations on 18 April 1944, with a Lancaster silhouetted above the target area.
(Courtesy IX Squadron Archives)

1945, and while Hitler was not in residence at the time it was still considered a success. The same day saw Lancasters take off for the last raid by the type, a night op to attack an oil target at Tønsberg in Norway on 25/26 April.

Lancasters not only made a vital and hugely significant contribution to Bomber Command's night offensive; they also helped to turn the tide in the major land battles of 1944 by bombing the German army in the field, and flying tactical sorties aimed at precision targets. Overall, during the war Lancasters had carried out around 156,000 sorties and dropped 608,612 tons of bombs.

In addition, before the German surrender, Lancasters were heavily involved in Operation Manna, which saw them supplying much-needed

A dramatic photograph of a 9 Sqn Lancaster east of Boulogne on a daylight ground-support operation on 17 September 1944.
(Courtesy IX Squadron Archives)

Lancaster B.I (Special) PB995 with a 22,000lb Grand Slam slung below. This Lanc was one of two trial B.I (Specials).
(Key Collection)

food to starving Dutch people. These sorties were potentially hazardous as large areas of the country were still under German control – though with war's end in sight a truce was negotiated and the Lancs were allowed to carry out their vital relief effort largely unhindered. Some 6,684 tons of food were dropped during 2,835 sorties.

Following the end of hostilities in Europe, Lancasters were also employed in another passive role. The bombers were used to repatriate liberated Allied prisoners of war back to England, the task being named Operation Exodus.

In the immediate postwar years a number of Bomber Command units remained equipped with the Lanc until the type was replaced by the Avro Lincoln. The last bomber unit to operate the type, 49 Sqn, converted to Lincolns in March 1950.

With the departure of the lend-lease Consolidated Liberators after the war, the Lancaster became the principal land-based maritime reconnaissance aircraft used by Coastal Command. The last example of the type to be operated in service by the RAF was MR.3 RF325, which was used by the School of Maritime Reconnaissance at RAF St Mawgan in Cornwall, and was retired on 15 October 1956. Sadly, after a farewell ceremony it was flown away to Wroughton, Wiltshire, to be scrapped.

The Lancaster also formally served with some other countries after the war. With the Royal Canadian Air Force the type continued to fly for some twenty years, operating in a variety of roles including air-sea rescue. The air forces of Argentina and Egypt also used the Lanc, as well as the French Navy. The Soviet Air Force assembled two examples from those that had force-landed in Russia during the first of the *Tirpitz* raids, the Royal Australian Air Force had two Lancs on its books, and the Swedish Air Force also used one as an engine test bed. Many Lancasters were also used in experimental and development trials, and some were put onto the civilian registers of Britain and Canada.

CHAPTER 2

PA474 – Battle of Britain Memorial Flight

PA474 was built as a B.I by Vickers-Armstrong at Hawarden, North Wales, in 1945. Initially, it was earmarked for 'Tiger Force' operations, and thus service in the Far East, so was manufactured to FE standards. However, the war with Japan ended before the Lanc could take part in any hostilities.

Instead it went into storage at 38 Maintenance Unit, Llandow, South Wales, on 18 August 1945. The Lanc was next moved to 32 Maintenance Unit at St Athan, also in South Wales, on 26 November 1946. After this period in storage PA474 was converted to PR.1 configuration by Armstrong Whitworth, with work beginning on 28 June 1947. The conversion included the removal of the Lancaster's turrets. The former bomber was ferried back to Llandow on 11 August and temporarily placed back into store. At some point during the work the aircraft's camouflage paintwork was stripped, leaving it with a bare metal finish.

On 23 September 1948, PA474 at last entered service with the RAF when it was assigned to 'B' Flight of 82 Sqn for photographic-reconnaissance duties in East and South Africa. After arrival with the squadron at Benson, Oxfordshire, it was

given the identification letter 'M'. The Lanc spent the next four years carrying out survey work. This saw its crews take PA474 on many detachments to small airfields with relatively primitive facilities. It returned to Benson on 18 February 1952 to await a fairly uncertain future.

The bomber's long-term fate became even more doubtful when, from 26 May 1952, PA474 was loaned to Flight Refuelling Ltd at Tarrant Rushton, Dorset, the intention being to convert the Lanc into a pilotless drone. Much design work followed while PA474 languished somewhat forgotten at Tarrant Rushton. However, before

PA474 while serving with 82 Sqn in Africa. The Lanc is pictured towards the end of its survey duties of East Africa with a flat tyre at Tabora, Tanzania, in 1952. While in this area 82 Sqn's northern detachment photographed an area of 30,000 square miles on the eastern side of Lake Tanganyika. Generally, the serviceability of PA474 during this period was excellent: on turnaround, after a 12- to 14-hour photo mission, its ground crew recall it as being a case of 'Just fill her up and go!'
(Pete Day)

The ultimate classic BBMF three-ship formation: the Lanc with Hurricane II LF363 and Spitfire II P7350. Whatever other wartime period paint schemes are chosen, the BBMF will always aim to retain these two fighters in representative Battle of Britain identities.

LF363 represents Hurricane I, R4197 US-C, of 56 Sqn, while P7350 – the oldest airworthy Spitfire and a genuine veteran of the Battle – is seen in the guise of Mk.I, L1067 XT-D *Blue Peter*, of 603 (County of Edinburgh) Sqn. *(Crown Copyright/MOD)*

this proposed work had begun the Air Ministry made a decision to use an Avro Lincoln instead.

So, on 7 March 1954, PA474 was transferred to the College of Aeronautics at Cranfield, Bedfordshire, where it was to be used for trials with several experimental aerofoil sections including the Handley Page laminar flow wing. This new career effectively saved an airworthy Lanc for the nation.

For this work, trial wings were mounted vertically on the upper rear fuselage of the aircraft, which at the time was still wearing its 82 Sqn badges and individual 'M' code. PA474 was used to test a number of aerofoil sections, actual and theoretical, for aerodynamic research. The aircraft was used in this role until 1964, by which time the College of Aeronautics had completed the conversion of Lincoln B.2 G-36-3 (the former RF342). During October 1963 the RAF had talked to the college about taking back PA474, with a view to putting it on display in the then-planned RAF Museum.

On 22 April 1964, the Lanc was ferried to 15 Maintenance Unit at Wroughton, Wiltshire, and

What effectively saved an airworthy Lancaster for the nation – PA474's time spent carrying out aerofoil experiments with the College of Aeronautics at Cranfield. Note that the Lanc still carries its 82 Sqn individual code letter 'M'.
(College of Aeronautics)

placed into storage. The RAF had regained this airworthy Lancaster and the first steps to it becoming a permanent flying memorial to Bomber Command had successfully been taken.

The aircraft was adopted by the Air Historical Branch with the intention of including it in the new museum. It was soon painted into a more fitting wartime camouflage paint scheme, though without any squadron markings. While at Wroughton, PA474 appeared in two films: *Operation Crossbow* and *The Guns of Navarone*. On 25 September 1964, PA474 moved to RAF Henlow, Bedfordshire, to be prepared for the RAF Museum.

The first unit to be equipped with Lancasters was 44 (Rhodesia) Sqn. In 1965 Wg Cdr M.A. D'Arcy, the Commanding Officer of 44 Sqn, which was by then flying Avro Vulcans from RAF Waddington in Lincolnshire, asked permission for PA474 to be transferred into the care of the squadron. It was promised that the aircraft would be stored inside a hangar at Waddington and also that a start could be made on the restoration work required for its eventual display in the museum.

With this in mind, the Lanc was inspected and found to be so structurally sound that rather than move the aircraft by road it was to be flown! Permission was granted for the bomber to make a single flight from Henlow to Waddington, but it was subsequently discovered that the tail wheel assembly was cracked. Also outside at Henlow was Lincoln RF398 (now on display at the RAF Museum Cosford, Shropshire), so one lunchtime the two Avro bombers were jacked up and after much hurried activity PA474's tail sat on a serviceable wheel assembly courtesy of its younger cousin!

At 1200hrs on 18 August 1965, PA474 took off from Henlow and set a course for Lincolnshire – the spiritual home of Bomber

Opposite: PA474 en route from Henlow to Waddington on 18 August 1965 during its 'one flight only'. The camera ship for this air-to-air photo was a Chipmunk flown by Vulcan pilot Fg Off Brian Fogg; at the time the 'Chippie' was being used to fly Air Training Corps cadets on summer camp at 'Waddo'. As so often happens on occasions such as this, the weather on that day had been wonderful until the Lanc approached Waddington, whereupon a bank of 'clag' formed out of nowhere. Again, in typical style the patch of poor weather conditions cleared soon after PA474 touched down!
(Brian Goulding)

An unusual view of PA474 in flight from below and aft, highlighting the form of the bomber very well.
(Duncan Cubitt)

On its starboard forward fuselage PA474 still proudly wears the *City of Lincoln* name and coat of arms.

Command. Before landing at Waddington the Lancaster carried out two flypasts at Scampton, Lincolnshire, the second of which included a steep turn over the station's then gate guard, Lancaster I R5868 (now at the RAF Museum London, see Chapter 6).

At Waddington PA474 was given the 44 Sqn markings KM-B, commemorating Sqn Ldr John Nettleton VC and R5508, the Lancaster he flew on the Augsburg raid of 17 April 1942. A restoration programme then began that would continue for many years.

By 1966 work was progressing well and both the front and rear turrets were in place. In 1967 PA474 was granted permission to fly regularly,

though the restoration work to bring the bomber up to the desired condition to accurately represent a wartime Lanc went on.

In the years immediately following the Second World War, it had become traditional for a Hawker Hurricane and Supermarine Spitfire to lead the Victory Day flypast over London. This regular tradition led to the idea of forming a collection of airworthy historic aircraft, initially to commemorate the RAF's major battle honour, the Battle of Britain. Later this would broaden into paying tribute to the RAF's role in other major battles of the war.

So it was that in 1957 the Historic Aircraft Flight was formed at Biggin Hill, Kent, with one

Hurricane (LF363) and three Spitfire XIXs (PM631, PS853 and PS915). Over the following years the Flight experienced variable fortunes and a number of moves. In 1973 there was a change of name as the Historic Aircraft Flight became the Battle of Britain Memorial Flight. PA474 joined the BBMF in November of that year. Then in 1975 the Lanc was adopted by the City of Lincoln, whose name and coat of arms it still proudly wears thirty years later.

The charter for the adoption reads:

WHEREAS during the years of the Second World War strong links were established between the Citizens of Lincoln and the personnel of RAF Bomber Command by reason of the proximity of the City and many operational bases

AND WHEREAS one aircraft remains airworthy typifying the many which flew from Lincolnshire at that time and it is the wish of the Citizens of Lincoln expressed most notably by the Lincolnshire Lancaster Appeal Committee that this long and continuing association should be formally recognised

NOW THEREFORE the City of Lincoln acting by the Council of the said City HEREBY ADOPTS

LANCASTER BOMBER PA474 bearing the name 'The City of Lincoln' and displaying the arms thereof: with the intent that so often as may be the said aircraft may be seen in the skies of Lincolnshire as a reminder to all of past efforts and sacrifices made in the cause of freedom.

The BBMF moved to its current home at RAF Coningsby, Lincolnshire, in 1976. Restoration work was still ongoing at the time, and a mid-upper turret that had been discovered in Argentina was finally fitted to the Lanc the same year.

PA474 was marked up as KM-B until 1979. Following the 1979 display season, the bomber was flown to Lyneham, Wiltshire, where it was given the AJ-G code of 617 Sqn's ED932. This was the Lancaster famously flown by Wg Cdr Guy Gibson VC, DSO*, DFC*, during the Dam Busters raid of 16/17 May 1943.

A few years later, having undergone a major servicing at St Athan during the winter of 1983/4, PA474 was painted as SR-D to represent an aircraft of 101 Sqn. PA474's next major service was contracted out to West Country Air Services at Exeter, Devon. It returned to Coningsby in March 1988 wearing the PM-M^2 code of ED888 while it was with 103 Sqn. During its service life with 103 and 576 Sqns this aircraft completed 140 operations – more than any other Lancaster. Due to the huge array of operations symbols, the coat of arms and *City of Lincoln* name were reduced in size and moved further forward.

With the frequency of the Lancaster's major servicing extended to six years, it was not until

When PA474 was first put back into the air by the RAF, it lacked a mid-upper turret. This was resolved in 1976 soon after the BBMF's move to Coningsby. The bomber is seen here wearing the markings of Sqn Ldr John Nettleton's KM-B.
(Author's Collection)

PA474 seen displaying at Alconbury in 1982. At this time the Lanc wore the 617 Sqn code AJ-G, representing the aircraft famously flown by Wg Cdr Guy Gibson on the Dam Busters raid of 16/17 May 1943. This picture captures the Lancaster's undercarriage in the process of being retracted, at such a point that it almost suggests the silhouette of an Upkeep being held in place below.
(Duncan Cubitt)

the winter of 1993/4 that PA474 received its next repaint. Carried out at St Athan, this saw the bomber applied with the markings of 9 Sqn's W4964 WS-J with its distinctive Johnnie Walker nose art and 'Still Going Strong' slogan – and representing another Lancaster centenarian. This Lanc had been a veteran of 106 ops, the 100th of which saw it drop a Tallboy bomb aimed at the mighty German battleship *Tirpitz* on 15 September 1944. The size and colourful nose art of the aircraft represented meant that this time the coat of arms and *City of Lincoln* name had to be moved to the Lancaster's starboard side.

On 25 September 1995, having completed that year's display season, PA474 set off from Coningsby and flew to St Athan ready to undergo a major wing re-spar programme. This had never been done before; the lifespan of a wartime Lanc was only expected to be relatively short, so there had really not been any need to consider that the type would ever need replacement wing spars.

A fatigue meter had been fitted on board PA474 when it joined BBMF. By the end of the 1983 flying season readings showed that the bomber had clocked up 3,060 hours, leaving 1,340 hours or about thirteen years remaining based on the usage at the time. In 1984 British Aerospace (BAe) determined the fatigue index to be 70.7, where an index of 100 indicates no fatigue life remaining. A decision to replace the spar booms was made in 1990, and BAe was tasked to define the repair, which was originally planned to be carried out during the aircraft's 1993–4 major service.

The intention of the repair design was to replicate as much of the historic concept of the Lancaster as possible. This included the use of a unique method of attaching the skins to the boom on the outer wings, known as

From 1994 until 1999, PA474 represented W4964 WS-J of 9 Sqn, wearing the well-known 'Johnnie Walker' nose art of this Lancaster centenarian.
(Duncan Cubitt)

plug riveting. However, the repair would not in any way compromise modern-day design practices and fatigue-enhancement measures.

The new booms were to be manufactured from extrusions surplus to the re-sparring programme of the RAF's Avro Shackletons. They were to be made without drilling any holes so that the drilling pattern could be copied from the existing booms. Additionally, the repairs were also required to include new webs and fasteners and new shackles.

There was a change of plan in October 1992, when a decision was made to keep the Lanc flying for as long as there was sufficient fatigue life available, which by then had been calculated to expire in 1996. Flying restrictions were imposed on the aircraft to avoid any heavy manoeuvres, and fatigue meter readings were regularly sent to BAe for analysis.

As the booms were the critical components they were wisely manufactured well in advance of the repair date and consequently completed in December 1993. Later, it was agreed that the repair work would be performed by BAe at Chadderton, near Manchester. In July 1995 BAe formally accepted the contract to carry out the Lancaster's re-sparring.

After its arrival at St Athan on 25 September 1995, PA474's engines and undercarriage were removed, then the airframe was separated and prepared for transportation. That November various sections of the aircraft arrived at BAe and were placed into purpose-built holding fixtures to support them during the work. Around 5,000 production hours were spent on the aircraft, by both military and civilian engineers who were often working from seven-thirty in the morning until eight o'clock at night, before completed sections were ready to make their way back to St Athan during early February 1996.

At St Athan the bomber was reassembled, and its first flight test was carried out on 13 May

PA474 at St Athan in October 1995, part-way through disassembly in readiness for its major resparring programme by British Aerospace. Here the engines and outer wings have been removed.
(Steve Fletcher)

Right: Starboard fin and rudder, with *Mickey's* 'M' identification letter prominently applied.

Below: Wartime picture of the original EE176 *Mickey the Moocher*. While serving with 61 Sqn, this Lanc amassed well over 100 operations, including 15 to Berlin. *(Via BBMF)*

with Flt Lt Mike Chatterton as captain. Two days later PA474 returned to Coningsby with its new spar in place – the still has several thousand hours of flying time remaining on it, so will see the Lanc fit to fly well into this new millennium.

The Lancaster received its popular 'Mickey the Moocher' paint scheme following another scheduled maintenance at St Athan, ready for the 2000 season. It was still wearing this for 2005. This identity represents 61 Sqn Lancaster III EE176 QR-M, a particularly notable example, being another of the relatively few Lancasters to survive in excess of 100 missions during the Second World War (EE176 is thought to have flown between 115 and 128 operations).

Although aircraft lettered 'M' were usually known as 'Mike' or 'Mother', one of EE176's crews called it 'Mickey' and adorned the bomber's port forward fuselage with the artwork

of Walt Disney's Mickey Mouse. Mickey was painted pulling a bomb trolley with a bomb resting on it, and the name 'Mickey the Moocher' was applied too – a parody of the popular song of the time 'Minnie the Moocher'. In front of the character is a signpost with two arms, the top one of which reads '3 Reich' and the other 'Berlin', presumably denoting where 'Mickey' was heading with his 'bomb' – EE176's target was Berlin on fifteen occasions.

Bomb symbols were then added behind Mickey for each op in rows of ten, and after five such rows a second column began aft of the first. Once that was complete, a third column appeared with five bombs in each row. It is here that the confusion creeps in as to how many operations were actually carried out by EE176 and how many were marked up. PA474 is annotated with 112 such symbols, placing it at a point in time just before the confusion begins.

The next major inspection of the Lanc is due during the winter of 2006–7. This will see the bomber take on a new identity, though we will just have to wait and see which famous Lancaster will live to fly again courtesy of PA474!

Since its formation the BBMF has emerged as one of the world's best-known and most respected collections of historic aircraft. Nowadays the Flight's display aircraft comprise the Lancaster, a Douglas Dakota III (ZA947), two Hurricane IIcs (LF363 and PZ865) and five Spitfires (Mk.IIa P7350, Mk.Vb AB910, LF.IXe MK356 and PR.XIXs PM631 and PS915). It also has two DHC Chipmunks (WG486 and WK518) on its books, which are used for conversion and continuation training of BBMF pilots on tail-wheel aircraft. Recent years have also seen Spitfire XVI TE311 undergoing restoration as a spare fuselage for the Flight.

Since the Flight's inception in 1957 its aircrew have been volunteers, all of whom nowadays perform primary duties on front-line types such

as the BAe Harrier GR.7 (gradually being upgraded to GR.9), Panavia Tornado F.3 and Boeing E-3D Sentry, or training aircraft like the Shorts Tucano and Hawker Siddeley Dominie. The only exception to this is the BBMF's Officer Commanding, who, with the additional demands of overseeing operations, administration and engineering, needs to be full time on the Flight. OC BBMF is assisted by a reserve officer as operations officer/adjutant and a civilian administrative officer.

Early on in the Flight's history the engineers, as with the aircrew, made themselves available on a voluntary basis. However, with the expansion of the Flight in the mid-1970s there was a need for a more formal engineering structure. Nowadays the BBMF has twenty-five full-time personnel under the control of a Warrant Officer as Engineering Officer, supported by a Chief Technician as Engineering Controller. These personnel handle

Once OC BBMF has worked tirelessly to plan the forthcoming season and ensure that the Flight's assets will be utilised to their best effect, the flying programme will be plotted up. Operations Officer Flt Lt Jack Hawkins is seen writing in the slot time of the entry for the Lancaster, a Hurricane and a Spitfire to fly from Southampton to Jersey on 9 May during the 2005 season. The following day's entry shows a take-off from Jersey at 1120hrs, with a flypast at Sark en route home to Coningsby, where the landing time is scheduled for 1310hrs.

all aspects of the maintenance of the fleet, not only at Coningsby but also out on the display circuit. The only aspect which is usually contracted out to industry is scheduled major servicing.

Records show that for many years after its formation the Flight carried out relatively low-key operations, generally performing around fifty to sixty displays a year up until the mid-1960s. This gradually grew, and by 1992 the participations had risen to about 150 per season, rising further to 200 in 1995 and exceeding 500 appearances for the 1996 season. During the 2002 and 2003 seasons, the BBMF amassed an incredible tally of over 600 individual aircraft appearances. At the start of the 2004 season this already impressive commitment had risen to a planned 700-plus individual appearances, with the BBMF booked to display at over 60 air shows plus 300 other events – and remember this is with

Looking out over Nos 3 and 4 engines as the BBMF bomber cruises over the English countryside.

Lincolnshire's Lancaster Association 2004 Open Day at Coningsby from the ground . . . (Crown Copyright/MOD)

just nine display aircraft! This demand shows no signs of declining; in fact, it just gets busier, with such a massive number of appearances now being considered the norm for the Flight, and bids for its aircraft to appear continued apace prior to the 2005 season.

A typical year will see the BBMF's pre-season work-up well under way during March, with PA474 having usually flown its first air test of the year sometime around the middle of the month. Any minor 'snags' arising during the test flight are rectified soon afterwards.

... and from the air, viewed from the tail gunner's turret with Hurricane IIc PZ865 (centre) and four Spitfires (from left to right: LF.IXe MK356, Mk.IIa P7350, Mk.Vb AB910 and PR.XIX PS915) caught flying over the BBMF hangar at Coningsby. *(Crown Copyright/MOD)*

A lovely study of the RAF's last remaining Lancaster at work in the skies of Great Britain, honouring the personnel of Bomber Command. *(Crown Copyright/MOD)*

The Air Officer Commanding's check is then generally scheduled for mid- to late April, where the Flight carries out its display routines for each type. Once happy with this the AOC will then give the BBMF the necessary authorisation for the season's displays. All being well, the Flight will usually begin public appearances with the Lanc during late April, and traditionally finish the year's flying at the Lincolnshire's Lancaster Association members' event, which is held at Coningsby during late September. The aircraft's appearances can be at locations throughout the UK mainland and surrounding islands: from Cornwall to Scotland, in Jersey and Guernsey, in Northern Ireland and occasionally even the near Continent in countries such as France and The Netherlands.

Due to its exclusivity and appeal, the Lancaster has become the flagship of the Royal Air Force's Battle of Britain Memorial Flight. The aircraft's popularity in the UK is unsurpassed; its displays and flypasts generally being followed by a

spontaneous round of applause from those on the ground. It is simply marvellous that the RAF still has a Lancaster on its books to act as a flying tribute to the Bomber Command crews of the Second World War. The Lanc has gained a tremendously high profile in the UK, often appearing on national TV as it carries out its many memorial, ceremonial and state duties.

I can say with some certainty that everybody just loves to see a flypast or display by PA474. But while we gaze in awe at this airborne tribute, it's all too easy to forget exactly what is involved in putting on the sequence we are seeing. So a description of a typical BBMF display routine and some of the procedures that see it get airborne might be helpful.

Firstly, it is important to state that PA474 is, of course, flown to the strictest of limitations and standards and always to visual flight rules (VFR). Being an aircraft owned and operated by the military, it has to comply with current RAF regulations. It is also very important to state that the Lancaster is part of a memorial flight, *not* a display team – the primary aim is to keep it flying for as long as possible. During the course of a season the BBMF Lanc will clock up an average of between 85 and 100 hours' flying time, but is limited to *no more* than 100. To further conserve the airframe's fatigue life, there is a maximum 'g' loading of 1.5g and a 'never exceed' limit of 1.8g.

The pilots also operate to strict crosswind limitations for take-offs and landings. This is limited to 10 knots initially, until the pilot has reached 50 hours on the aircraft, whereupon he may take off in crosswinds of up to 15 knots, which is PA474's permitted maximum.

Take-offs are timed quite precisely so that as many displays and flypasts as possible can be fitted into the 100 hours. Before a display or flypast the navigator will have carefully worked out a flight plan that will see the Lanc arrive at the relevant venue exactly on time.

If you've ever visited the BBMF's home at Coningsby to see PA474 set off on a sortie, or been at an air show where the Lancaster has landed and you have subsequently watched it start up, you might have noticed that the No. 3 engine (starboard inner) is first to be fired up. This is because the aircraft's inboard engines each have a 1,500 watt DC generator.

At this point it may also be worth noting the fuel tanks and capacity for PA474. The Lanc has

With external power connected, PA474 is all ready for start-up at Coningsby.

For start-up a 'very rich' mixture is used. When the chemically correct amount of fuel is supplied to burn all the oxygen in the air it is called a 'normal' mixture; when there is excess fuel it is called a 'rich' mixture; and when there is less fuel it becomes a 'weak' mixture. The mixture of fuel and air is designed to vary with the differing conditions under which the engine will operate. Starting: 'Very rich' – extra fuel is supplied by a separate pump to ensure vaporisation. Slow Running: 'Rich' – with the engine at idle the mixture is rich, and when brought to normal running it will accelerate. When the throttle is opened the air responds first by bringing the mixture to normal, and this prevents the engine from weak cutting. Economical cruising: 'Weak' – for economy, a mixture is required which ensures that all the fuel is burnt; to do this there must be excess air. Rated or Maximum Continuous Power: 'Slightly rich' – to obtain maximum power all the oxygen in the air must be burnt; to achieve this a little extra fuel is required. Take-off power: 'Very rich' – to keep the engine and installation weight to a minimum the engine cooling system is designed to keep the engine just at the correct running temperature at rated power. When extra power is required through increasing engine speed and manifold pressure, the engine cooling system cannot keep the engine within working temperatures. To overcome this, extra fuel is supplied which vaporises and cools the cylinder; it cannot burn, as there is insufficient oxygen. If the engine is not cooled in this way, detonation ('pinking') may occur at high manifold pressures. Mixture strength on PA474 is auto-matically controlled by boost pressure, and there is no separate mixture control.

the standard fuel-tank configuration for the type, which comprises two No. 1 tanks (580 gallons each), two No. 2 tanks (383 gallons each) and two No. 3 tanks (114 gallons each). The No. 1 tanks are located within the inner wing sections, one on each side of the fuselage. Nos 2 and 3 tanks on each side are located in the outer wing sections, one either side of the outboard engine nacelle. PA474's normal fuel loading is 850 gallons, distributed thus: 125 gallons in each of the No. 1 tanks, 200 gallons in each of the No. 2s and 100 gallons in each of the No. 3 tanks.

The fuel used for PA474 is AVGAS 100LL. The former NATO code for AVGAS was F18, although that term is now obsolete. Nowadays the engines are operated with 100 octane petrol (low lead), whereas towards the end of the Second World War, and after it for a time, there was the benefit of ratings up to 150 octane using tetraethyl lead to boost the octane. However, the way that the BBMF use the engines, at only relatively low boost settings (approximately half of what is available), detonation or 'pinking' caused by high boost pressures with low-octane fuel is not a problem; the high boosts that were used operationally are not needed to fly the Lancaster in its current role.

The starting checks go: 'Brakes – on; ground/flight switch – as required; flying controls – full and free; undercarriage – down and bolted. Two greens; radios – on and checked. Frequency selected; fuel – No. 2 tanks selected; master cocks

One for technically minded readers to lose themselves in! An underside view of the No. 2 engine minus cowlings. Each of the Lancaster's four Rolls-Royce Merlins has its own oil system (37½ gallons of OM270, including 2 gallons for propeller feathering, plus an air space of 4½ gallons), its own cooling system (30:70 mix of AL3/distilled water) and its own electric starter.

– off; ladder – stowed; helmets – on. Crew check in; G4B inverter – on; throttles – ½ inch open. Friction set; RPM levers – maximum friction set; radio – start clearance if required; start No. 3 engine; anti-collision lights – on; master cock – on; ignition switches – on; clearance – clear No. 3. Turn No. 3; fire warning light – out; oil pressure – rising; RPM – 1,200; bomb doors – closed; start No. 4 engine; start No. 2 engine; start No. 1 engine. Starting checks complete.'

Once all four engines have been started, the after-starting checks have been carried out and the crew are ready, the pre-taxi checks will be carried out: 'Engine temperatures and pressures – within limits; radiator shutters – open; pneumatic pressure – checking reading; ladder – stowed; door – closed and unlocked; taxi clearance – obtained; altimeters – set. Compared; chocks – removed; fuel flow – complete positive flow checked. Pre-taxi checks complete.'

With all this carried out, the engines are brought up to 1,200rpm and PA474 rolls towards the relevant active runway. There are then a total of eighteen pre-take-off checks which must be carried out on the Lanc, including the engine run-ups and mag-drop checks; hence the bomber sits into wind for some time before take-off.

While we are all patiently waiting for the throttles to be opened, inside the Lanc things are getting very busy. 'Flight instruments – checked, vacuum reading; trimmers – zero, neutral, set for take-off; ignition switches – on and caged; throttle friction – set; RPM levers – maximum, friction set; pneumatic pressure – reading; engine temperatures and pressures – within limits; pressure head heater – on; fuel – master cocks on; No. . . . tanks selected. Nos 1 and 2 tanks booster pumps on. Crossfeed cock – off; flaps – 20 degrees down indicating, selector neutral; radiator shutters – automatic; superchargers – M gear; compass – checked and compared; direction indicator – set and uncaged; hatches and

windows – secure, closed; harnesses – tight and locked; take-off weight – . . . lb; take-off brief – complete.' Once all these checks have been carried out and everything is OK, the navigator will call 'Pre-take-off checks complete'.

If the display is a three-ship with one each of the BBMF's Hurricanes and Spitfires, the take-off sequence will usually be Spitfire, Hurricane, then Lancaster. Once the Lancaster's crew see the Hurricane start to roll, boost will be set to zero. When the Hurricane is airborne the bomber's brakes will be released and the captain will call for settings of 3,000rpm and +7 boost. The crew make a final check of the instruments and they're off.

As PA474 rolls and gains speed, after around just twelve seconds the tail will be lifted. The Lanc will normally rotate at 90 knots, which takes just over 30 seconds to reach. Then it's straight into the after-take-off checks: 'Brakes – on, off; undercarriage – up. Lights out; climbing power – set; engine temperatures and pressures – checked; flaps – up, indicating. Selector neutral; door – closed and locked. After-take-off checks complete.'

The reason the brakes are briefly touched before the undercarriage is retracted is to stop the wheels rotating after the take-off roll. Once the undercarriage is up the aircraft maintains a shallow rate of climb until its speed builds. The Lanc will be travelling at about 120 knots at a height of 150ft when the captain calls for flaps up. The fighters will soon join up in a loose formation and transit speed to a display venue is usually 150 knots, with the Lancaster's engines running at around 2,000rpm and zero boost.

In operation the piston engine is subject to two separate stresses. Inertia stresses are caused by the speed at which it rotates (RPM). Gas pressure stresses are caused by the manifold air pressure, or 'boost', as it is more commonly known.

Consequently, the two main power ratings of the engine involve changes in both RPM

Battle of Britain veteran Spitfire P7350 dominates this impressive photo of the classic BBMF three-ship formation, with Hurricane LF363 and Lancaster PA474 further from the camera. *(Crown Copyright/MOD)*

and boost. For this purpose there are two controls fitted in the cockpit – the RPM lever and the boost lever, or throttle. The RPM lever is connected via the constant-speed unit to control the pitch of the propeller, while the throttle is connected to the engine to control fuel flow and consequently the power delivered by the engine. Generally speaking, 1in of boost alters the aircraft's speed by about 10 knots.

On arrival at the display venue, the BBMF will perform a three-ship formation flypast in front of the crowd at between 150 and 170 knots, at 300ft. As they reach the end of the crowd line, the Lancaster's navigator will call 'Fighters, break, break, go!'

The two fighters will then peel off, and the 'Spit' will commence its solo display. Meanwhile, the Hurricane will hold to the rear of the display site at 1,500ft, with the Lanc doing likewise behind the crowd at 1,000ft. While in a holding pattern, the Lanc crew will monitor the fighter displays in order that they are ready for their cue to begin the display. After the Spitfire comes the Hurricane's display, whose pilot will give a radio call one minute before the end of his routine, whereupon PA474 will be positioned ready for its first flypast.

As the Hurricane carries out the final manoeuvre in its sequence – a climbing victory roll at 600ft – the Lanc will have commenced its first flypast at 100ft, with the engines set at 2,400rpm and zero boost, resulting in a speed of 180 knots. The 'nav' starts his stopwatch as the

Above: With the engines set at 3,000rpm and +7 boost, on the take-off roll PA474's tail wheel lifts after just 12 seconds. The Lanc will normally rotate at 90 knots, which takes just over 30 seconds to reach. Here the bomber is seen departing Fairford, Gloucestershire, after its appearance in the special '100 Years of Flight' static line-up at the 2003 Royal International Air Tattoo in July. *(Steve Fletcher)*

Below: To the right of the captain's seat are the undercarriage and flaps controls, plus the trim-tab wheels. The large red lever in the curved housing at the far left is the undercarriage control. The silver bolt with a red lever retaining the main control is the undercarriage-control safety bolt. Forward of these, the large brown wheel is the elevator trim-tab control; behind that, pointing upwards is the rudder trim-tab control; and the wheel positioned at the front of this box is the aileron trim-tab control. The D-ring at the front of all these controls is the flaps selector.

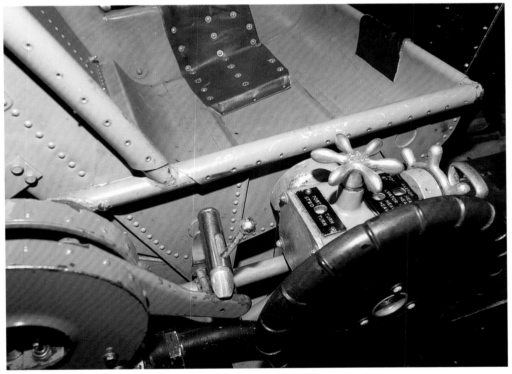

bomber passes the datum point, and the crew count to eleven seconds for still air (though this may be adjusted depending on the length of the crowd line and the strength of the wind) before pulling up and away to reduce the speed to around 150 knots. The co-pilot then reduces the boost to -4, as the nav opens the bomb-bay doors.

As the Lancaster approaches the display datum again, it commences a 360-degree turn at 300ft to offer the crowd a good view of the bomb bay. The speed comes down to 130 knots, with the aircraft climbing to 400ft during the far part of the turn. The bomb-bay doors are then closed and the bomber continues the turn 'clean'.

Having passed the datum again, with PA474 flying away from the crowd, the captain checks for speed below 150 knots and calls for flaps to 20 degrees. The undercarriage is lowered and as the aircraft returns to its audience the engines are increased to 2,850rpm. The navigator gives the fighters a 'one minute rejoin' radio call and the Lancaster's gear-down pass is carried out at 110 knots, at a height of 100ft.

On passing the datum the brakes are briefly applied to stop the wheels turning in the wind, then released again. The captain calls for gear up, and as the wheels are retracted he calls for +7 boost as the bomber turns away from the crowd. At 120 knots the flaps are retracted and the Lanc accelerates towards 150 knots, with the power reset to 2,000rpm at +4 boost. As this happens the two fighters have caught up and are rejoining in formation. Due to its lower stalling speed, the Hurricane always rejoins on the inside of the turn. Once both fighters are in position on either side of the bomber, they call in and the three-ship formation will come around for one more pass. Turning at 140 to 150 knots, PA474 leads the formation along the display line at 300ft to exit in the opposite direction from which it arrived. Dependent on wind strength and the venue, a

typical BBMF Lancaster display will last for approximately five minutes.

If it is to land at an airfield where an air show is taking place, you'll note that the Lanc touches down using a 'wheel it on' approach, rather than the 'three-pointer' type landing used during the war. The downwind leg is flown at 2,400rpm and zero boost, which gives a speed of around 140 knots. The pre-landing checks are carried out: 'Flaps – 20 degrees down indicating, selector neutral; undercarriage – down and bolted. Two greens; RPM levers – 2,400; fuel – contents checked. No. . . . tanks selected. Nos 1 and 2 booster pumps on; superchargers – M gear; brakes – parking brakes off. System reading – zero at wheels; harnesses – tight and locked. Pre-landing checks complete.'

By the end of the downwind leg the speed will have been reduced to 115 knots. Turning onto finals, the flaps will be lowered to 40 degrees and the engines will be brought up to 2,850rpm, with the boost remaining at zero. Power is reduced in increments of 2in of boost, and the Lanc approaches the threshold at 90 knots with a setting of -6 boost. Once safely down the engines are 'slow cut' and the flaps raised. Bringing up the flaps reduces lift, provides more air over the rudders, giving better directional control, and prevents the Lanc from being skittish during the landing.

After-landing checks and engine run-down drills are then carried out: 'Radiator shutters – open; flaps – up. Selector neutral; RPM levers – maximum; booster pumps – off; pressure head heater – off; brakes – pressure reading . . . After-landing checks complete.' The run-down drill follows: 'Ignition – dead and live check carried out; boost – static check; ignition – check. Run-down drill complete.'

With the bomber in its parking position, the crew go through the shut-down checks: 'Bomb doors – as required; master cocks Nos 1, 3 and 4 engines – off; flaps – fully down; master cock No. 2 engine – off; ignition switches – off (when propeller stopped); undercarriage indicator – off; flaps – operated. Selector neutral. Indicator off; anti-collision lights – off. Fuel – all cocks off; radiator shutters – automatic; direction indicator – caged; navigation equipment – off; radios – off; electrical services – off; chocks – in position port and starboard; brakes – off; ground/flight switch – ground; hydraulic accumulator – reading . . . (220psi). Shut-down checks complete.'

As mentioned earlier, the BBMF's primary role is just as its name suggests, a Memorial Flight. In recent years PA474 has been involved in some very prominent flypasts on memorial, ceremonial and state occasions, and I'd like to describe a selection of these in greater detail to offer a flavour of what's involved in carrying out such duties.

The funeral of Her Majesty Queen Elizabeth the Queen Mother in London on 9 April 2002 caught the attention, and stirred the emotions, of the whole nation. The Queen Mother personified the wartime spirit that helped Britain win through the Second World War, and thus a flypast of her funeral cortège by the Battle of Britain Memorial Flight was wholly appropriate on a day so rich with symbolism.

As patron of the Battle of Britain Fighter Association, the Queen Mother had also written the Foreword in the BBMF's 2002 brochure. Some words quoted from Her Majesty's message in the brochure are tremendously relevant for mention at this point: 'It remains as true today as it was in 1940 that the price of peace is eternal vigilance and to that end the Royal Air Force is deployed and engaged in theatres throughout the world in defence of peace and security. The aircraft of the Memorial Flight provide a tangible link between "The Few", the crews of Bomber Command who paid such a heavy price, and their counterparts of today.'

PA474, flanked by PM631 and PS915, flies over Buckingham Palace with its Union Flag at half mast out of respect for the Queen Mother on 9 April 2002.
(Crown Copyright/MOD)

So it was wholly fitting that part of the 'Tay Bridge' Operation Order, which outlined the details of the Queen Mother's funeral, included provision for a flypast of BBMF aircraft. However, had it not been for a fortunate spell of good springtime weather that year this may not have been possible – the BBMF's principal operating season is from May until September – and thus they could easily have been excluded from the proceedings.

At the time the Flight was in its pre-season work-up period at their Coningsby base, and the then OC BBMF, Sqn Ldr Paul Day OBE AFC (well known to many as 'the Major'), was fortunately in a position to be able to offer PA474 and two Spitfires when approached by 1 Gp on 4 April. This was possible because the Lanc had performed a completely successful air test that same day and needed no rectification work, and also by virtue of the fair weather that had allowed the fighter pilots to carry out a number of Spitfire currency sorties.

The BBMF Lancaster and two
Spitfire PR.XIXs overfly the
Queen Mother's funeral cortège
as it proceeds down The Mall on
9 April 2002.
(Crown Copyright/MOD)

Taking part in the flypast with the Lancaster would be the Flight's two PR.XIXs, PM631 and PS915. The former would be making its public debut in a new 541 Sqn paint scheme, which saw it retain photographic reconnaissance blue, though this time with invasion stripes and standard RAF blue and red roundels rather than the South East Asia Command roundels it had formerly worn. The reason that a Hurricane was not part of the flypast, which would of course have been a more representative BBMF formation, was simply that Mk.IIc LF363 – the only one of the Flight's two examples that was airworthy at that point – was considered by Sqn Ldr Day not to be cosmetically acceptable for a public display, let alone a state occasion such as this.

Leading the formation in PM631 was Sqn Ldr Day, with PS915 flown by Sqn Ldr Clive Rowley MBE who is now OC BBMF, having taken over from the Major for the start of the 2004 season. Crewing the Lancaster were Sqn Ldr Stuart Reid (captain), Flt Lt Andy Sell (co-pilot), Sqn Ldr Brian Clark (navigator) and Flt Sgt Ian Woolley (air engineer).

The original order asked for a flypast of Parliament Square at 1121hr, though when the Assistant Chief of the Air Staff went to see the Royal Family on 6 April it was requested that the flypast coincide with the funeral cortège being halfway down The Mall. It should also be pointed out that only ACAS has the authority to allow single-engined aircraft to fly over London for an occasion such as this. The new plan required a different holding point (with provision for flexibility in the timing) and run-in route, but arrangements were soon in place to ensure this could be carried out smoothly.

Once the cortège left Westminster Abbey following the funeral service, it should have taken precisely 7½ minutes to be halfway down The Mall, where the flypast was to coincide with it.

On 17 May 2003 PA474 re-creates a scene from sixty years earlier, as it flies over Eyebrook Reservoir, one of the sites used by 617 Sqn to train for the dams raid.
(Duncan Cubitt)

Pre-flight brief at Waddington, as navigator Flt Lt Garry Simm (far right) details the route for the Dam Busters 60th anniversary flypasts to the rest of the aircrew. From left to right they are: Sgt Marv Parsons (air engineer); Sqn Ldr Bob Sutton (navigator); Sqn Ldr Stu Reid (captain); and Flt Lt Ed Straw (co-pilot).

With no guarantee as to precisely what time the Queen Mother's hearse would leave Westminster Abbey, though, a 1 Gp staff officer on the ground was in radio communication with the formation to give them their cue.

As it happened the procession ran slower than anticipated, and when the BBMF aircraft reached their position, with precise timing to the second, the cortège had only reached Admiralty Arch. A snap decision was therefore taken to make a second pass in order to ensure the flypast coincided with the procession being halfway down The Mall on the approach to Buckingham Palace. The formation turned 180 degrees, flew downwind for one minute then turned to position themselves for the second run – and as they flew over Admiralty Arch they saw that the cortège was now in the correct position. As the BBMF overflew the hearse at 1,000ft, the Spitfires dipped their wings as a salute to the Queen Mother –

while the huge crowds who had made the trip to London to pay their respects gazed in admiration.

Given the importance of this occasion, it was entirely appropriate that the decision was taken to go round again. The Queen was seen looking up emotionally at the flypast as the historic aircraft passed overhead to pay the RAF's tribute to her mother.

The aircraft were waved off and greeted on their return back at Coningsby by large crowds along the outside of the perimeter fence, many of whom were waving Union Flags to mark the occasion for which the Flight's aircraft had taken to the air. It was therefore most considerate of the crews to take the time to go over to the fence and talk to the spectators when they had returned from the flypast, a typically understanding gesture from the BBMF personnel. Touches such as this one make these occasions even more memorable for the enthusiastic spectators.

All the BBMF personnel were quite rightly very proud of the part they had played in such a historic occasion. The aircraft are so synonymous with a time when the Queen Mother refused to leave London, instead offering her support to victims of the Blitz, that their appearance added a very special tribute to her. Sqn Ldr Day and his staff certainly went to great lengths to ensure their obligation was entirely fulfilled, and this day immediately went down as one of the most memorable in the Flight's history.

Another memorable occasion involved the Flight commemorating one of the Lanc's finest hours. Most people, whether fascinated by our aviation heritage or not, have heard of the famous dam busters raid of 16/17 May 1943. This legendary raid just about made a place for the Lancaster and its crews in British folklore. It was further turned into legend after the release of the 1955 blockbuster film *The Dam Busters*. Starring Richard Todd OBE as Wg Cdr Guy Gibson, to this day the film remains one of the most enduring war films of all time and is consequently still regularly screened on television.

May 2003 saw the 60th anniversary of the raid, which once again brought about renewed interest in Operation Chastise. In order that the occasion should be commemorated in fine style, the BBMF's Lancaster was naturally requested to perform flypasts over several relevant sites. These were scheduled to include Eyebrook Reservoir in Rutland, the Kent coast just off Reculver, Brooklands in Surrey and Scampton in Lincolnshire; however, Brooklands unfortunately had to be missed out due to very poor weather conditions in the London area.

Indeed, sixty years to the day later, on 17 May, the weather conditions were nowhere near as favourable for the commemorative flypasts as they had been on the clear night of the mission itself. Had it not been for the determination of the

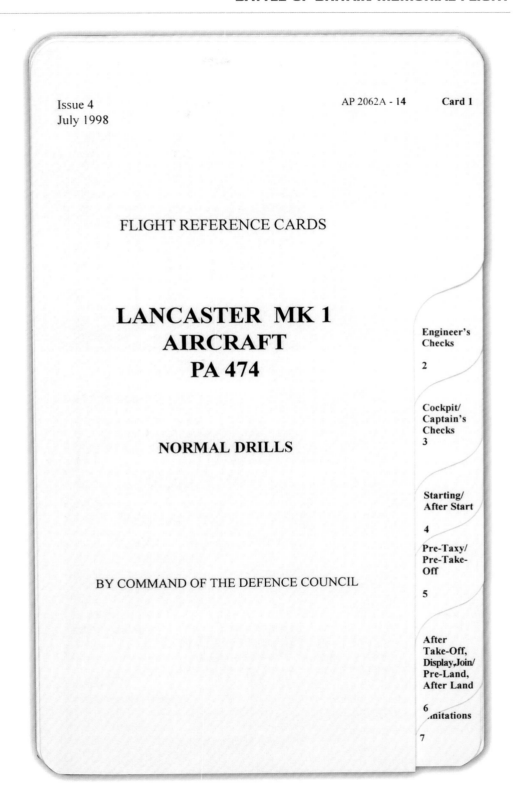

FLIGHT REFERENCE CARDS

LANCASTER MK 1 AIRCRAFT PA 474

NORMAL DRILLS

BY COMMAND OF THE DEFENCE COUNCIL

Issue 4
July 1998

AP 2062A - 14   Card 1

Engineer's Checks

2

Cockpit/ Captain's Checks

3

Starting/ After Start

4

Pre-Taxy/ Pre-Take-Off

5

After Take-Off, Display, Join/ Pre-Land, After Land

6

Limitations

7

Undergoing scheduled winter maintenance inside the BBMF's hangar at Coningsby during January 2005. Rolls-Royce Merlin types fitted to PA474 at the beginning of the 2005 season were: No. 1 – Merlin 502; No. 2 – Merlin 225; No. 3 – Merlin 25; and No. 4 – Merlin T24.

PA474 has all the standard crew positions, the only significant difference from an operational Lancaster's wartime configuration being the dual control arrangement for the pilots.

An almost timeless image as PA474 is caught above an unspoilt area of English countryside. In general each of the Lancaster's Merlins consumes approximately 50 gallons of fuel per hour – so when that figure is multiplied by four it becomes apparent why the BBMF always work towards getting the maximum efficiency out of the engines. The aim of 'cruise control' for any aircraft is to travel as many miles as possible on one unit of fuel. With a piston engine this is achieved by selecting the appropriate supercharger gear and then setting a medium boost with low RPM. This method of operation is not only the most economical, though; it also results in less vibration, which in turn reduces airframe fatigue and engine noise. All this also makes transit flights more comfortable and less tiring for the pilots.
(Crown Copyright/MOD)

Lancaster's crew to make sure the tribute was paid – and that the countless people making trips out to view the Lanc were not disappointed – the sortie could well have been cancelled. Aircrew consisted of Sqn Ldr Stuart Reid (captain) and Flt Lt Ed Straw (co-pilot), Flt Lt Garry Simm (navigator) and Sgt Marv Parsons (flight engineer).

The crew had been calling for Met information since 0700hrs, and were soon made aware that they had to get the Lanc out of Coningsby as soon as possible because crosswinds were nearing the 'out of limits' mark. On arrival at the BBMF hangar during the late morning of 17 May, they made the decision to fly to nearby Waddington where the runway would be suitably aligned for a take-off with the wind blowing in the direction it

was. By 1200hrs the Lanc was taxiing out at Coningsby, and took off with a 14-knot crosswind – and remember, the limit is 15 knots! A short while later it was on the ground at Waddington and the crew were preparing for the sortie.

Inside Waddington's ops room the crew briefed for the flight. This was to be a lengthy trip, also

Navigator Sqn Ldr Jeff Hesketh monitors the progress of a sortie with a VFR chart, notepad and pen, portable GPS and stopwatch.

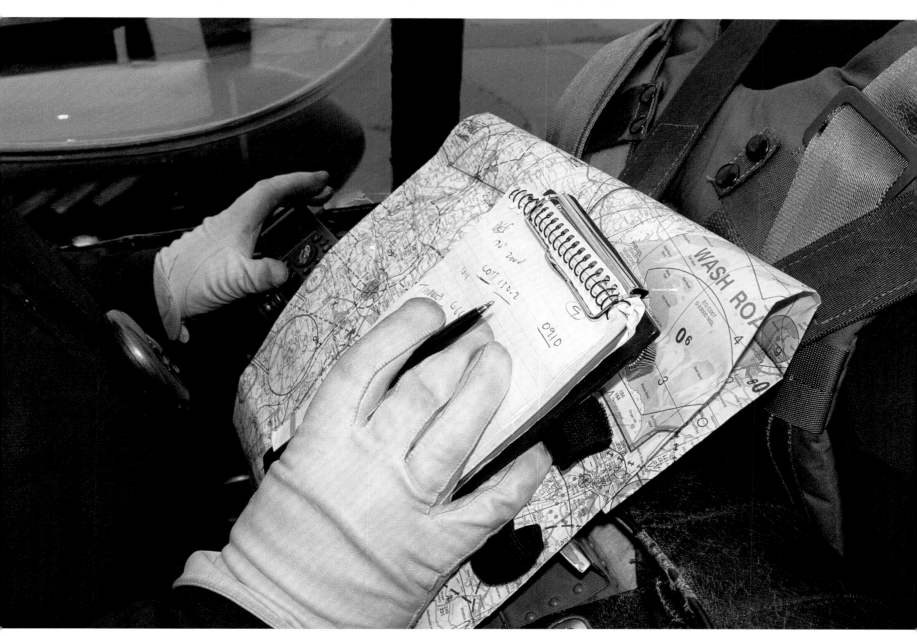

After PA474 has taxied back to the BBMF hangar and arrived in its parking position, navigator Sqn Ldr Jeff Hesketh goes through the engine shut-down checks.

With some 617 Sqn veterans watching out back, and many more out front, the Petwood Hotel at Woodhall Spa is overflown by PA474 en route to Coningsby on the 60th anniversary of the Dam Busters raid.

including a flypast at Bletchley Park and a display at Brands Hatch motor-racing circuit. And at Eyebrook there was to be additional participation by BBMF fighters and two Panavia Tornado GR.4s from 617 Sqn. Take-off from Waddington was set for 1405hrs.

That day, Waddington was hosting 44 (Rhodesia) Sqn Association's annual general meeting. The chance for the members to watch a Lancaster firing up at Waddington, the first RAF base to receive the type, put former BBMF pilot Flt Lt Mike Chatterton's illustrated talk about flying the Lanc behind schedule: 'I can't compete with that,' Mike commented. Waddington was also on the list of flypasts by virtue of the AGM, and once it had got airborne the sight of PA474 flying overhead was much appreciated by all the veterans present at this former Second World War Lancaster base, which was also the site where the restored bomber had begun its new lease of life with the RAF.

The first series of flypasts was to take place at Eyebrook Reservoir, two miles south of Uppingham. From 4 May 1943, during the final stages of training for Operation Chastise, this reservoir sometimes saw as many as nine 617 Sqn Lancasters at a time operating above it, initially at 150ft, but after 5 May going down to just 60ft and at a ground speed of exactly 232mph.

Featuring a straight dam at its southern end, and full of water in May, Eyebrook was ideal for the squadron's training. White canvas targets were erected on the dam wall on 4 May, grouped in twos linked with camouflage scrim, and spaced to simulate the towers of the Möhne Dam in Germany. Initially, the local inhabitants feared all the noise was coming from German bombers attacking, but gradually they became used to the

Opposite: Inside the Petwood Hotel after the anniversary flypasts, dams raid pilot Les Munro tells the BBMF Lancaster crew about his experiences of flying over Uppingham Lake.

repeated low flying and even gathered in the lanes round about to watch as the Lancs pulled up sharply over the dam and fired flares. It is also interesting to note that Eyebrook is referred to as Uppingham Lake in contemporary Operation Chastise documents and pilots' logbooks. Just 48 hours before Chastise, all nineteen available Type 464 Provisioning Lancaster B.IIIs took off and flew as a squadron for the last time before the operation. On this final exercise, Wg Cdr Guy Gibson took off at around 2150hrs on a sortie which lasted 3 hours 5 minutes. He noted in his logbook: 'Full dress rehearsal on Uppingham Lake and Colchester Reservoir. Completely successful.' Gibson also made a note about the reservoir in his book *Enemy Coast Ahead*: 'for the Möhne Lake we had Uppingham Reservoir, which was much the same shape though, of course, much smaller.'

For the 60th anniversary tribute, PA474 was cleared for three flypasts at 250ft over the reservoir and dam, to be followed by the BBMF fighters 30 seconds behind. Initially, it was planned that a Hurricane and one of the Flight's Spitfires would take part, though once again the weather took a hand.

Prepped and ready to go for the trip were Spitfire II P7350 and Mk.V AB910. However, these Spitfire variants are restricted to 10-knot crosswind take-offs, and consequently were out of limits on this particular day. Instead Wg Cdr Paul Willis, who at the time was Coningsby's Station Commander, had to take Hurricane II LF363 aloft on its own in order to ensure a BBMF fighter presence.

After the BBMF flypasts, 617 Sqn provided a brace of Tornado GR.4s to fly over Eyebrook Reservoir. Wg Cdr Dave Robertson, OC 617 Sqn at the time, made a special trip to Rutland to watch. The roads around the reservoir were three deep with cars. Many, many people had come to witness this occasion – some at the north end of

Right: View of the wreath-laying ceremony at the National Memorial to the Battle of Britain, on 26 September 2003, from the bomb aimer's position of PA474.

Opposite: This map shows the amount of detail required for the BBMF to carry out a flypast exactly on time, in this case over the National Memorial to the Battle of Britain at Capel le Ferne, near Folkestone, Kent, as planned by navigator Sqn Ldr Jeff Hesketh. The red arrow at the bottom shows the direction of the Lancaster's arrival. The black square around the motorway junction denotes the IP (Initial Point), and there is a 'trombone' (oval track) at this point to enable the time to be adjusted if necessary. Arriving at the IP at 1007hrs 45secs, the straight black line, on a magnetic track of 087°, is followed for 2 mins 15 secs to make the first flypast over the target within the black triangle at precisely 1010hrs. This run-in begins at the standard cruise rate of 150 knots ground speed, accelerating to 170 knots. The five marks on the track are timing points, which due to the aircraft's acceleration along the track are not exactly at equal intervals in time. The red times give 'clock time' for the first of three flypasts to occur at 1010hrs (local). The circle to the right of the target denotes the area where the Lancaster's turns could be made to position it ready for the subsequent flypasts. The red arrow pointing away from the target represents the bomber's exit direction after the last flypast on a magnetic track of 330°. *(Reproduced from Ordnance Survey mapping on behalf of Her Majesty's Stationery Office – © Crown Copyright 100043870 2005)*

the reservoir, some elsewhere around it, and some on the wall of the dam itself.

Next on the agenda was Reculver, on the North Kent coast. Barnes Wallis himself stood at Reculver to watch Upkeep trials, making it a most appropriate location for a commemorative flypast. The first inert gas-filled Upkeep cylinders dropped by 617 Sqn were released at Reculver on 11 May 1943. Three Type 464 Provisioning Lancasters 'attacked' simulated targets on the promenade there and rolled practice bombs up the beach. Over the following days until 14 May, further 617 Sqn aircraft performed similar drops. These tests proved to Barnes Wallis and the aircrew that the strict release constraints of the Upkeep could be achieved with remarkable accuracy.

As the BBMF's Lanc headed along its planned flight path over the sea off the Isle of Sheppey just to the north of Whitstable and Herne Bay, it became apparent to the crew that this part of the Kent coastline was also crammed with thousands of eager spectators. The degree of public interest meant that the roads leading to Reculver had to be closed off as the location reached capacity.

Among the crowds at Reculver's well-known 'twin towers' was Barnes Wallis' son Christopher, who was in the area to open a new permanent Dam Busters exhibition at the Herne Bay Museum and Gallery. This was how the request for the flypast came about. The exhibition features photos and information on the dams raid, the Dam Busters, Barnes Wallis, testing at Reculver and how the bombs worked. There is also an audio-visual display, an especially good way of providing children with this information.

A very personal connection with this area comes through one of the dams raid pilots, Plt Off Warner H.T. Ottley DFC, who originated from Herne Bay. 'Bill' Ottley was the pilot of Avro Lancaster B.III (Special) ED910 AJ-C on Operation Chastise, and was shot down to the

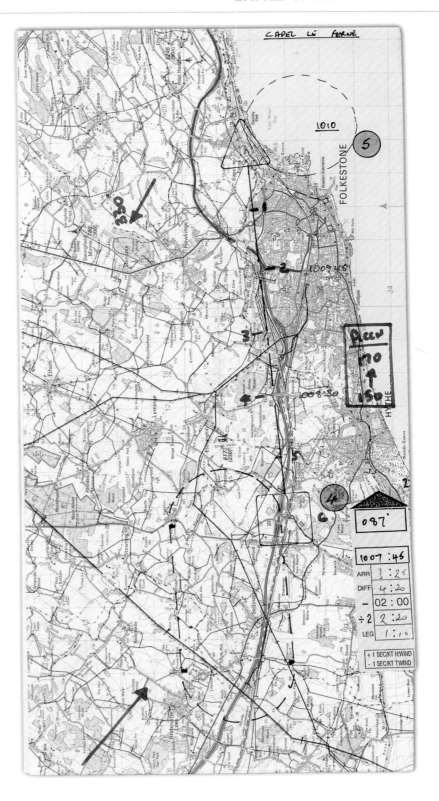

Right: Heading for home from a trip to Kent, the view from the bomb aimer's position of PA474 as the Lanc approaches the Queen Elizabeth Bridge at Dartford.

Opposite: Approach into Barkston Heath's runway 24 for a 'hangar break'.

north of Hamm, Germany, crashing at 0235hrs on 17 May 1943 on his way to the Lister Dam. Only one member of his crew survived, and Plt Off Ottley was posthumously awarded the Distinguished Flying Cross for his previous service with 207 Sqn. With the local connection in mind, the museum's new exhibition featured a picture of the town's 'Dam Buster'. Reculver played such a major role in the run-up to the famous raid that seeing the Lancaster flying over this bouncing bomb test site was a very fitting local tribute.

Next, the route was scheduled to take in the Brooklands Museum at Weybridge, where a Dam Busters 60th Anniversary Salute was being held. Barnes Wallis spent much of his working career at Weybridge, and on that day the museum was opening a special exhibition about the scientific work he did for Vickers-Armstrong at Brooklands during the Second World War.

Unfortunately, though, the awful wet weather on the day finally got the better of the Lanc, and despite a number of determined attempts the crew reluctantly decided it was not possible to get around the west side of London. They therefore had to turn back, navigate to the Queen Elizabeth Bridge at Dartford, and head north to their next port of call for the tribute – Scampton.

This, of course, was the base from which 617 Sqn had set out on Operation Chastise. Today it is home to the RAF's famous aerobatic display team, the Red Arrows, and Guy Gibson's much-loved pet Labrador, Nigger, is still buried there outside his former office in front of No. 2 Hangar.

Possibly the most appropriate occasion on this memorable day was the 617 Sqn Aircrew Association 60th anniversary dams raid dinner, held at the well-known Petwood Hotel in Woodhall Spa, Lincolnshire, where later in the war the squadron's officers were billeted while stationed at the nearby RAF base.

The list of attendees was astounding. Present were two former aircrew who flew on Operation

The BBMF Lanc at Coningsby after a busy weekend of displays on 4/5 September 2004, including flypasts at IWM Duxford in front of a number of 9 and 617 Sqn veterans of the *Tirpitz* raids to mark the 60th anniversary of that mission.

While PA474 is painted to represent significant wartime Lancasters, standard BBMF operating procedures see it retain its correct serial number and not assume that of the identity taken on.

Chastise, Sqn Ldr Les Munro DSO, QSO, DFC, the last surviving pilot from the raid, and Sqn Ldr George 'Johnnie' Johnson DFM, bomb aimer on ED825 AJ-T and a sergeant at the time. Guest of honour was the then Chief of the Air Staff, ACM Sir Peter Squire GCB, DFC, AFC, accompanied by Lady Squire. Another prominent guest was Richard Todd, who as mentioned earlier played the leading role of Wg Cdr Guy Gibson in *The Dam Busters* film. The total complement was made up of veterans of the squadron from throughout its history – from the dams and *Tirpitz* raids to the Vulcan era – plus a number of local dignitaries, serving RAF officers and specially invited guests.

On its way back from Scampton to Coningsby the Lanc performed another tribute to the veterans as it flew over the Petwood Hotel. Former aircrew moved outside for a better view as they heard the sound of the Rolls-Royce Merlins.

But the day's events didn't quite finish there. Flt Lt Ed Straw had been in touch with 617 Sqn Aircrew Association members and asked if the BBMF crew could visit the Petwood Hotel to meet some of the veterans when the day's duties

BBMF Bomber Leader Sqn Ldr Stu Reid at the controls of PA474 heading north back towards Lincolnshire.

were over. They were happy to oblige, and Sqn Ldr Stu Reid, Flt Lt Ed Straw and Flt Lt Garry Simm went along to the Petwood before dinner began. It must have been fascinating and a real privilege to listen to Les Munro telling the BBMF crew about his wartime experiences flying a Lancaster over Uppingham Lake at just 60ft, at night!

The following morning there was a commemorative flypast over the impressive 617 Sqn memorial at Woodhall Spa. As the veterans stood in front of the monument, which represents a breached dam, four 617 Squadron Tornados were followed by PA474, flying a final tribute on this anniversary weekend.

The way this memorable weekend turned out proved that the exploits of the Dam Busters are held in as high regard nowadays as they have ever been. The story's hold on public imagination was made evident from the enormous numbers who turned out in adverse weather conditions to see the commemorative flypasts by the RAF's last remaining Lancaster. Personally, I could not have imagined a more fitting tribute to the Dam Busters, and indeed to all the members of Bomber Command, than what had taken place for this 60th anniversary.

It was really brought home to me just what it had all meant when one former Lancaster pilot at the Petwood Hotel commented to the BBMF crew: 'I heard the Merlins and for a moment I was airborne again.'

My first flight on board a Lancaster came on 26 September 2003. This sortie was to be a flypast by the Lancaster over the National Memorial to the Battle of Britain at Capel le Ferne, Kent. The memorial has a reputation as being an emotive place to visit, and I had long been planning to go there to see it for myself – though I could never have anticipated viewing it from the air in the bomb aimer's position of the BBMF Lancaster!

Each year a Memorial Day is held at Capel le Ferne. This generally takes place on the Sunday closest to 10 July and is attended by around 350 paying guests, plus VIPs and veterans. There are flypasts by various aircraft, normally including some from the Battle of Britain Memorial Flight. With the Battle of Britain Memorial theme, it is usual that a Hurricane and Spitfire from the BBMF take part. But in September 2003 there was also a flypast over the Battle of Britain Memorial by the BBMF's Lancaster. On the ground on this day wreaths were to be laid on the memorial in honour of 'The Few' by an Air Training Corps squadron.

At the time the BBMF aircraft were still temporarily outbased at Barkston Heath, Lincolnshire. The Flight's aircraft had moved there during early June 2003, as the runway at Coningsby was to be resurfaced during the summer in readiness for the arrival of the RAF's new Eurofighter Typhoons.

First in to the airfield were Hurricane II PZ865 and Spitfire II P7350, which made the move on 8 June. These were joined later the same day by PA474 and Spitfire V AB910, both arriving directly after displaying at the Biggin Hill International Air Fair that weekend. Most of the Flight's other aircraft arrived at Barkston the following week.

The flypast at Capel le Ferne was scheduled for 1010hr, and as the memorial site was exactly an hour's flying time away for the bomber, take-off was set for 0910hrs. As captain, BBMF Bomber Leader Sqn Ldr Stu Reid carried out the pre-flight brief, detailing the crew, the route and all emergency diversions, and so on, in case a problem should occur. With the Lanc prepared for flight, the crew carried out the walk-round checks at 0845hrs. The aircrew consisted of pilots Sqn Ldr Stu Reid and Flt Lt Ed Straw, navigator Sqn Ldr Jeff Hesketh and flight engineer Flt Sgt Andy Barlex.

Pre-start checks were carried out and the engines fired-up at 0855hrs. PA474 taxied out to Barkston's runway 24, and held while the crew carried out the pre-take-off checks. Then, at precisely 0910hrs the brakes were released and the engines smoothly increased to 3,000rpm and +7 boost, and the Lancaster was soon airborne.

En route to Capel the Lancaster flew over Stamford, Lincolnshire, crossed the north–south running A1 road and then turned to port to fly around the western side of RAF Wittering. It continued south past Grafham Water in Cambridgeshire, and tracked down along the length of the A1 until it was in the vicinity of

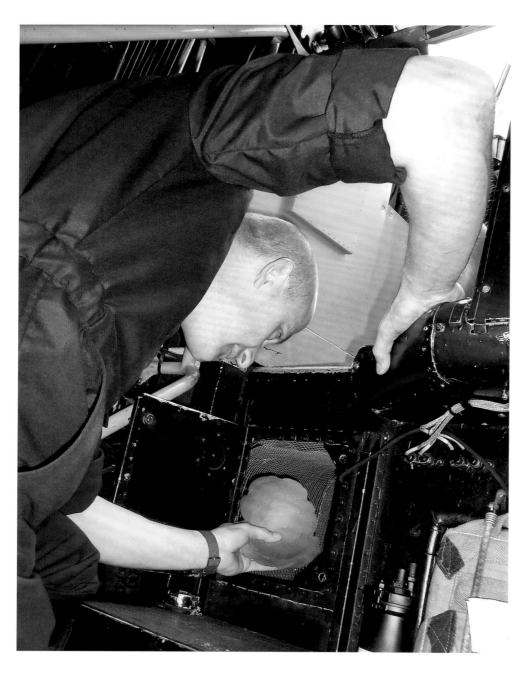

BBMF Airframes Technician J/T Chris Elcock loads the last handful of 1 million poppies into PA474's bomb bay on 3 June 2004.

London, flying over the prominent landmark of the Queen Elizabeth Bridge at Dartford, Kent, as it headed towards Rochester.

A course was then flown parallel to the route of the M20, past Ashford, to take the bomber to meet up with the large roundabout at Junction 11 of the motorway close to Folkestone racecourse. This was where the navigator had plotted the IP (Initial Point). From there a track of 087 degrees running along the outskirts of Folkestone was taken, with five precise timing points marked on it.

The first flypast was made directly over the memorial from inland, and, typical of BBMF operations, was *precisely* on time. The Lanc then turned starboard out to sea, and came right around into position for a second pass over the clifftop memorial. PA474 then turned out over the Channel again and made a third and final pass, again from a seaward direction, though this time slightly to one side of the memorial, offering spectators on the ground a different view of it. This was a special tribute indeed, the BBMF's role making it particularly fitting to honour 'The Few' with a flypast by its flagship aircraft over this wonderful national memorial.

On arrival back at the BBMF's temporary airfield, PA474 went into circuit via what the BBMF call a 'hangar break' – PA474 having once again carried out its duty. It is worth noting that this was one of the Lancaster's last sorties out of Barkston; most of the Flight's aircraft returned home to Coningsby on 5 October 2003.

The RAF regularly pays its respects at this memorial, with flypasts not only by the BBMF but also by operational front-line squadrons. At the 2003 Memorial Day a Panavia Tornado F.3 from 56 Sqn, the unit with which Wg Cdr Geoffrey Page DSO, OBE, DFC* (whose idea the memorial was) had served during the Battle, passed overhead. This all serves to emphasise the site's enormous significance and the tremendous support it receives from the Royal Air Force.

Having flown over the site in one of the RAF's Memorial Flight aircraft, I felt compelled at last to make my planned visit to Capel le Ferne. It certainly is a humbling experience. After inspecting everything on the site, and spending a while beside the lone 'pilot' statue at its centre, I did indeed feel quite moved myself. I then went to inspect the visitors' remarks book to see what others had felt. Of the many comments, ones that sang out to me included, 'Will never be forgotten', 'God Bless them all', and 'A very moving experience'. The Battle of Britain Memorial is well recommended as a place to visit. And if you're lucky enough to be there when the

Merlins of the BBMF's aircraft fill the skies over the clifftops with their characteristic roar, just keep an eye on that lone pilot . . . is he glancing skywards for a moment thinking that one of his missing fellows has finally come home?

Part of the many commemorations for the 60th anniversary of D-Day during June 2004 included a poppy drop from PA474. The BBMF's part in commemorating the D-Day tributes was a complex five-day operation which included not only the Lanc, but also Dakota III ZA947 and Spitfires Vb AB910 and LF.IXe MK356. Of particular note, both these Spits actually took part in the D-Day operations – making their role in commemorating the 60th anniversary all the more poignant.

The view inside the Lancaster's bomb bay filled with approximately 1 million poppies. Note the wire sleeving put in place to protect the mechanical workings.

Poppies away! View from the rear gun turret as the poppies are dropped alongside the MV *Van Gogh* on 5 June 2004.
(Crown Copyright/MOD)

AB910 was flown by Fg Off George Lawson of 402 'Winnipeg Bear' Sqn RCAF on a beachhead cover patrol on 6 June 1944, from 0945hrs to 1215hrs. Later the same day, from 2200hrs to 2359hrs, it was flown by Plt Off H.C. Nicholson on a night beachhead cover patrol. On D-Day +1, Fg Off Lawson took off in AB910 at 0430hrs to carry out a dawn beachhead cover patrol. Just 2½ hours after landing, the Spit was up again for another similar duty piloted by Plt Off K.E. Heggie. AB910 flew two more operational sorties on 8 June, and four on 10 June.

MK356 was used on several fighter and fighter-bomber ops during the build up to D-Day. On D-Day +1, 7 June 1944, Fg Off Gordon E. Ockenden of 443 'Hornet' Squadron RCAF flew two patrols over France on invasion duties – the second of which was in MK356. During this sortie he was involved in a low-level attack on four Messerschmitt Bf 109Gs. Fg Off Ockenden gave chase to one of the 109s in the Spitfire IX, and obtained a shared victory after hitting it with a number of strikes. Today, MK356 wears the same markings as it wore during its participation in the invasion of France.

On 4 June 2004 the Lancaster and two Spitfires set off from Coningsby to pre-position at Southampton in Hampshire. As 5 June dawned, these three aircraft carried out a morning display over Portsmouth Harbour, from where a flotilla of vessels set sail to make their way to Normandy in a symbolic crossing of the Channel. These included cruise ships, historic vessels and multinational Navy ships. The same morning saw ZA947 head to Le Havre, France (where the Flight would be based for its 'detachment'), ready to load paratroops for a paradrop later in the day.

In the afternoon the Lancaster and Spitfires carried out another display, this time at the air show being held at Sandown on the Isle of Wight. After the display, the three BBMF aircraft continued on to carry out the poppy drop over the cruise liner MV *Van Gogh*.

Chartered by the Royal British Legion, the *Van Gogh* had on board it some 450 veterans who

Accompanied by a Spitfire on each side, the BBMF Lancaster D-Day 60th anniversary poppy drop viewed from sea level.
(*Crown Copyright/MOD*)

Flying Log & Fatigue Data Sheet

MOD Form 725(Lancaster) (Revised Aug 98)

Aircraft Serial No PA 474 — Sheet No 01

would take part in a memorial service en route to France. As the ship approached the French coast, at 1500hrs the service of preparation was to be relayed live on television. The service included a two-minute silence and culminated in wreaths being laid in the Channel from the ship's side. As a finale, at 1630hrs PA474, which had the two Spitfires in formation to each side of it, dropped a staggering 1 million poppies from its bomb bay alongside the ship.

The poppies were supplied by the Royal British Legion, and work to get them in place had taken the BBMF ground crew around a week. Preparations included the requirement to line the Lancaster's bomb bay with a protective sleeving, to safeguard the mechanical workings, before the poppies could be loaded – 1 million, by hand! The last poppy drop from PA474 prior to this was carried out in commemoration of the 50th anniversary of VJ-Day in 1995, and took place over The Mall, London.

There were further appearances by the BBMF aircraft on 6 June, the anniversary day itself. A highlight of the complex schedule was the participation of all four of the Flight's aircraft that had been deployed to France in a major flypast by British and French air forces, which included the RAF's Red Arrows, over the main anniversary ceremony at Arromanches. In attendance at this ceremony were seventeen heads of state, including Her Majesty Queen Elizabeth II.

The sorties outlined here are just a small sample of the range of duties undertaken by the BBMF during the course of a season. It is estimated that the Flight's aircraft will be seen by in the region of 6 million people each year. And long may this continue, as to see the Royal Air Force devoting these priceless assets to the memories of the airmen to whom we owe such a great debt just goes to demonstrate the Battle of Britain Memorial Flight's motto: 'Lest We Forget'.

BBMF Airframes Technician J/T Rachel Warnes applies a new poppy symbol to PA474 following the D-Day 60th anniversary, joining those for the D-Day 50th and VJ-Day 50th anniversary drops. PA474 also carried out a poppy drop earlier in its BBMF flying career when, at sunset on 4 May 1976, 10,000 petals were released from its flare chute during the dedication ceremony of the Dutch memorial to the crews of Bomber Command in the town of Dronten in The Netherlands. At the time the flare chute had only recently been fitted after being acquired from a retired Vickers Varsity which was about to be scrapped – and the Varsity's flare chute was virtually identical to that of the Lancaster.
(Crown Copyright/MOD)

Left: July 10 2005 was called National Commemoration Day, and was the last day in a week of events to mark the 60th anniversary of the end of the Second World War. The date was symbolic rather than historically significant, falling mid-way between VE-Day and VJ-Day. The grand finale of the commemorations was a flypast comprising a total of nineteen historic aircraft in five waves. The flypast was planned by the RAF's 2 Group Headquarters at High Wycombe, Buckinghamshire. Approval came from Air Marshal Clive Loader, Deputy Commander-in-Chief Strike Command. Taking off from Duxford, Cambridgeshire, during the Flying Legends airshow, the aircraft were to fly down the length of The Mall and over Buckingham Palace at 1,000ft, with the first wave scheduled to be in place at 1700hrs. With OC BBMF Sqn Ldr Clive Rowley MBE flying the Spitfire, and Sqn Ldr Al Pinner MBE in the Hurricane, the Lanc's aircrew consisted of captain Sqn Ldr Stu Reid, co-pilot Flt Lt Mike Leckey, navigator Sqn Ldr Dick George and air engineer Sqn Ldr Ian Morton. But also on board the Lanc was Marshal of the Royal Air Force Sir Michael Beetham. Sir Michael, now 82, had flown a Lancaster over Buckingham Palace as part of the 1946 Victory Parade. Her Majesty Queen Elizabeth II and the royal family were gathered on the Palace balcony to watch the event.
(Crown Copyright/MOD)

Opposite: The Lancaster's bomb bay was filled with 1 million poppies which were to be dropped as soon as the aircraft reached the Queen Victoria Monument directly in front of the Palace. It is estimated that 250,000 people turned out to see the flypast in London on National Commemoration Day. This is the view from the Lancaster's rear turret.
(Crown Copyright/MOD)

Right: For the National Commemoration Day flypast on 10 July 2005 the BBMF's Lancaster was flanked by Spitfire II P7350 to port and Hurricane II LF363 to starboard, the formation seen here about to fly over Buckingham Palace just before the Lanc released 1 million poppies from its bomb bay. *(Crown Copyright/MOD)*

With the top of the Queen Victoria Monument at far left, the BBMF formation leaves a trail of 1 million poppies in the blue skies over Buckingham Palace on National Commemoration Day. *(Crown Copyright/MOD)*

CHAPTER 3
FM213 –
Canadian Warplane
Heritage Museum

The world's two airworthy Lancasters differ significantly in one very important respect: Mk.X FM213 at the Canadian Warplane Heritage Museum, Hamilton, Ontario, is flown in civilian rather than military hands. Being such a rare and significant aircraft, keeping it in airworthy condition under civilian ownership involves a complex conundrum of logistical requirements.

But ever since its first post-restoration flight on 11 September 1988, the CWHM has been operating the Lanc to incredibly high standards that more than meet all the requirements. The bomber is now a 'living' memorial tribute to Plt Off Andrew Mynarski VC, a Canadian air gunner who was posthumously awarded the Victoria Cross for his selfless actions attempting to save the life of one of his crewmates on the night of 12/13 June 1944.

Keeping FM213 in the air has been an amazing achievement all round. The story of how the CWHM revived this once pole-mounted Lancaster, and how the museum continues to keep it airworthy today, truly deserves to be told in more detail. But first it might be useful to those who are slightly less familiar with the story of the Canadian-built Lancaster Xs to briefly outline how some 430 examples of this mark came to be manufactured in Canada.

As the war situation worsened during 1940, Britain and its Allies put plans in place to build as many aircraft as possible. And if their manufacture could be undertaken beyond the range of German bombers, so much the better. At the time the United States was not involved in the war, so Britain turned to Canada.

It was agreed that Avro Lancasters would be built at the National Steel Car Corporation's new aircraft plant in Malton, Ontario. The company had been more accustomed to working with railway rolling stock in Hamilton, but with the onset of war it received several orders to build aircraft. These included Martin B-26 Marauders and Westland Lysanders, the construction of wings for Handley Page Hampdens and Hawker Hurricanes, and the assembly of Avro Anson Is.

On 18 September 1941, a high-profile meeting took place in the offices of the British Supply Council in Washington DC to discuss the urgent need to build Lancasters in Canada. At this

meeting it was agreed that the Canadian order for 300 Marauders would be cancelled, and instead attention should turn to the production of Lancs. The order was announced that December and the first drawings arrived at Malton in January 1942. To act as a master-tool and pattern standard, Lancaster I R5727 was flown from England to Canada in late August 1942 – the first Lanc to cross the Atlantic.

The Canadian-built bombers were to be designated Lancaster Xs, and would predominantly be built to the same design and manufacture as the B.III. One of the biggest differences was that the Mk.Xs would be powered by Packard-built Merlin 224s, though early-built examples relied on Merlin 38s.

Additionally, to overcome a parts-supply problem, all instruments, radios and ball bearings would be supplied by Canadian or US companies. A completely new wiring system would also be included. However, it was necessary to ensure there would be inter-changeability of all major components between British and Canadian sub-assemblies so that modifications, repairs and battle-damage replacement could be carried out without having to ship parts across the Atlantic.

A staggering ½ million manufacturing processes were involved in building a Lancaster, which was made up of some 55,000 separate parts – even when you count engines and turrets as one item and exclude all the rivets, nuts and bolts.

Due to various management problems, the National Steel Car Company Aircraft Division was taken over by a Crown corporation and renamed Victory Aircraft. This company in turn later became A. V. Roe Canada Ltd.

KB700 was the first of the Canadian-built Lancasters. It carried out its maiden flight on 1 August 1943 – just over eighteen months after the drawings had arrived in Canada and a year after 'pattern' aircraft R5727 had flown in.

Marked up as KB726 VR-A, FM213 made its first post-restoration flight on 11 September 1988. The Lanc is caught here in superb fashion during an air-to-air sortie with its bomb doors open.
(Duncan Cubitt)

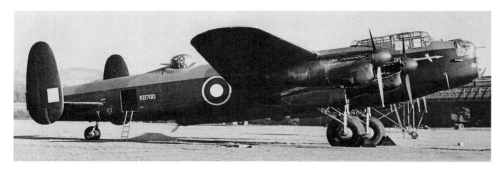

The first Canadian-built Lancaster X was KB700 *Ruhr Express*, which crashed on landing after returning home from its forty-ninth operation – it was due to be retired and sent back to Canada as a memorial aircraft after completing fifty ops. *(Key Collection)*

During a ceremony on 6 August, KB700 was famously christened *Ruhr Express*. Its name and nose art appeared on both sides of the forward fuselage.

A great deal of publicity surrounded KB700's naming, first flight and departure to England, where it arrived on 15 September. Initially, the Lanc served on 405 'Vancouver' Sqn RCAF at Gransden Lodge, Bedfordshire. This squadron was part of 8 (Pathfinder) Gp, and thus KB700 was the only Lancaster X to serve outside of 6 (RCAF) Gp under Bomber Command jurisdiction.

Hamilton, Ontario, is home to the Canadian Warplane Heritage Museum. This busy international airport handles much freight traffic, such as the UPS Boeing 757 seen in the background as 'KB726' prepares to taxi out.

Ruhr Express flew just two operations with 405 Sqn: one was aborted due an engine failure, while the other was a raid on Berlin. During late April 1944 the first Canadian Lanc was then transferred to 419 'Moose' Sqn, Middleton St George, County Durham.

On 2 January 1945, after completing its forty-ninth operation – on this occasion to Nuremberg – KB700 experienced hydraulic problems while attempting to land. The flaps would not lower properly and, after overshooting the runway, the bomber ended up in a farmer's field, where it collided with a piece of earthmoving machinery. The Lanc burst into flames, but despite the additional hazard of exploding ammunition all the crew miraculously escaped, though KB700 was destroyed.

Its loss was particularly sad, because at the time plans were being made to fly *Ruhr Express* back to Canada after its fiftieth operation. It was hoped that its triumphant return would act as a tribute to all the Canadians who built and flew Lancasters. At the same time, by the first quarter of 1945 production at Victory Aircraft Ltd had reached one Lanc per day – a task that employed around 10,000 people. In all, 430 Lancaster Xs were built.

The first order of 300 Mk.Xs, produced between August 1943 and March 1945, was allocated the serial numbers KB700 to KB999. Aircraft in the second batch were allocated FM100 to FM299; these were built from March 1945 onwards. However, with the war over, production stopped at FM229. The last Canadian

When FM213 is positioned as a static exhibit, the Canadian national flag and the RCAF ensign proudly fly from the Lanc.

'Defensive armament' fitted to FM213's turrets comprises dummy machine guns made by one of the museum's volunteers.

FM213 looking very purposeful with the sun shining directly on its nose.

Lanc rolled off the production line in September 1945.

Aircraft from KB855 onwards were supplied with Martin 250/CE Type 23A electric mid-upper turrets fitted with two Browning 0.5in machine guns, instead of the more familiar Frazer Nash FN-50 turrets with their two 0.303in guns. The Martin turrets were also positioned further forward on the fuselage.

The authorities in Britain were very impressed with the standard of workmanship. On arrival in the UK, KB705 was used on interchangeability trials, and it was found that all the major components were within the tolerances stipulated for the Canadian-manufactured aircraft. On acceptance in England, Lancaster Xs were assigned to 6 Gp, the Royal Canadian Air Force component of Bomber Command.

By war's end 105 Canadian-built Lancs had been lost in wartime service. Of these, approximately seventy per cent went missing in action and the other thirty crashed either on their return to England or during training. KB732 flew the most operations of any Canadian-built Lancaster, completing eighty-three missions during its tour with 419 Sqn. This Lanc survived the war, but was disposed of in May 1948.

Following victory in Europe, three Canadian Lanc squadrons (427, 433 and 434) became involved in ferrying prisoners of war home to England, many of whom were RCAF aircrew. With the war in the Pacific still ongoing, 160 Canadian Lancasters were flown back across the Atlantic to Nova Scotia to be prepared for service against the Japanese: 405, 408, 419, 420, 425, 428, 431 and 434 Sqns were allocated for the proposed 'Tiger Force', and returned to Canada to begin training with the Lancaster Xs in June 1945. But, of course, plans were cancelled following the surrender of Japan that August.

In the autumn of 1945, the roar of several squadrons of Lancasters was heard over southern Alberta, though only the once. Most of the British Commonwealth Air Training Plan bases had been closed by this time, and several were to be used as storage sites for the now-redundant bombers. Before landing their Lancs for the last time, the aircrews – in celebration of having survived the war – buzzed prairie towns and farms at extremely low level, frightening both residents and livestock! The Lancasters were then parked in long rows, the government unsure of what to do with them.

Many of the Lancs were sold to farmers for just a few hundred dollars each, their parts being put to various uses around the farm. Obviously their engine and hydraulic oil came in very useful, but the aircraft also provided a seemingly endless supply of wire, metal tubes and sheet aluminium.

Some of the more imaginative uses saw Lancaster tail wheels being fitted to threshing machines, bomb-bay doors acting as borders in flower gardens, propeller spinners being turned into plant pots, and escape hatches with windows helping to let a little light into outhouses!

However, in 1946 a more productive use was found for the Mk.Xs, and many of the 'low time' airframes were modified for service with the RCAF and given Arabic number designations. They were used for a variety of tasks, and during the course of being modified nine different versions were produced, with a new designation being given to unmodified examples. While some of these variants were produced in numbers, others involved just a single Lancaster.

The variants were: 10AR – Arctic Reconnaissance; 10BR – Bomber Reconnaissance; 10DC – Drone Carrying; 10MR/MP – Maritime Reconnaissance/Maritime Patrol; 10N – Navigation trainer; 100 – Avro Orenda engine test bed; 10P – Photographic Reconnaissance; 10S – Standard postwar bomber; 10SR – Air-Sea Rescue; and 10U – Unmodified wartime bomber.

In the late 1940s the international situation was again changing, as growing tension between the East and West culminated in the Berlin Airlift of 1948 and the creation of the Iron Curtain. One of Canada's responses was to modify a large number of its Lancs to become maritime reconnaissance/patrol aircraft to act primarily in the anti-submarine role.

Radar and sonobuoy operators' positions were installed in the rear of the fuselage, and the gun turrets were removed. A 400-gallon fuel tank was placed in the bomb bay to increase the Lancaster's patrol range. Also, due to the lengthy nature of the sorties, provision was made for a full-time co-pilot, and a cooking stove was installed in the centre section. Much upgraded electronics, radar and instrumentation were

bestowed on this variant, and a new 'Hi Viz' paint scheme completed the conversion. These Lancaster 10MR/MPs served throughout the 1950s until they were replaced by Lockheed Neptunes.

When the Lancasters were 'struck off strength' by the RCAF in the early 1960s, most were broken up and sold as scrap. The type was ceremoniously retired from RCAF service on 8 April 1964, at Downsview, Toronto, when FM104 and KB976 were overflown by KB882. A number of the recently retired

When the Canadian Lanc returns to Hamilton, it often does so by what is known in those parts as a 'museum arrival'. The result, as photographed here from the CWHM's high-level viewing balcony, is a pleasant view of the bomber's topsides.

This is a 'museum arrival' as viewed from on board the Lanc. The CWHM's ramp is visible behind the trailing edge of the wing; filled here with static aircraft on display outside for the Father's Day 'Soar with Legends' event on 18 June 2004. The museum's wonderfully shaped hangar dominates the view of the ground, with the high-level external viewing balcony noticeable on the ramp side. CWHM's car park is the one filled with a group of vehicles visible just to the side of the Lancaster's wingtip.

FM213 on search and rescue duties off the coast of Newfoundland during the latter part of its RCAF service years (probably early 1960s). *(Courtesy Canadian Warplane Heritage Museum)*

Lancs were given new duties as display aircraft, including FM104, which was placed on a plinth on Toronto Harbourfront.

Some Canadian-built Mk.Xs were also employed as transports, and later others even found their way into civilian hands. KB702 and 703 were converted into transports and operated by the Canadian Government's Trans-Atlantic Air Service from 1943 until 1947. And six specially modified Lancaster XPPs formed the fledgling Trans-Canada Airlines, and helped launch the era of mass air travel over the North Atlantic. Initially, the priority was to provide a mail service to the Canadian forces serving overseas and transport to key personnel on wartime assignments, before the service was expanded to include regular passenger flights.

Five Lancaster Xs were placed on the Canadian civil register. CF-IMF (FM222), CF-IMG (KB907) and CF-IMH (KB709) were used for survey work by Spartan Air Services Ltd, Ottawa. CF-KHH (FM208) was converted into a fuel-oil tanker and used by World Wide Airways to carry oil to the Arctic. CF-TQC (KB976) was converted into a water bomber, then later sold to the Strathallan Collection in 1975 and ferried to Scotland as G-BCOH in May of that year (KB976 is now located at Fantasy of Flight, Polk City, Florida, and is one of the ten Lancaster Xs that still survive).

FM213 was one of the last Lancaster Xs off the production line, being built in January 1945. Initially, it suffered from a number of snags and by the time it passed a further test flight on

31 August it was not needed for the war effort so was placed straight into storage.

It was taken on strength by the RCAF on 21 June 1946, though its conversion to 10MR/MP configuration was not completed until 1951. The Lanc was test-flown in its new form by de Havilland Canada test pilot George Neal on 16 December 1951. It was then allocated to serve on 405 Sqn based at Greenwood, Nova Scotia, and received the unit code AG-J.

However, en route to Greenwood the Lancaster's inexperienced ferry crew caused considerable damage during a heavy landing at Trenton, Ontario. On final approach the Lanc rounded out far too late and bounced straight back into the air. The throttles were opened up in an attempt to ease the aircraft back onto the runway, but on touching down at the second attempt FM213 bounced again – higher than the first time. On the third bounce the starboard tyre burst and the undercarriage collapsed.

The Lancaster then ground-looped and ended up in a snowbank facing in the opposite direction. It was thought at the time that the snow was responsible for there being no fire after the crash, as it had likely extinguished any flames and soaked up spilling fuel. The aircraft's centre section was severely damaged, however.

After its category 'B' crash, with just 10.5 hours' flying time on the clock, FM213 was dismantled and returned to storage with de Havilland at Downsview. It remained there for some time, while a replacement centre section was found. The RCAF approached de Havilland concerning the feasibility of repairing it. In turn de Havilland contacted Found Brothers Aviation Ltd, a company which had previously purchased many of the surplus Lancs, to see if a replacement centre section could be found. True to their name, Found Brothers knew the whereabouts of a Lancaster which had been bought from War Assets by a farmer near Penhold, Alberta. The

aircraft in question was KB895, and the farmer's intention was to convert the Lanc into a somewhat glamorous tool shed. He built three ramps and moved the bomber so as to have its main wheels sitting on the top of two piles of timber about 6ft high, with the rear fuselage supported in the air by a wooden 'X' frame.

KB895 sat like this for many years, and as time went on the farmer's interest in his ambitious project waned. As more time passed, the weight of the bomber began to push the piles of timber into the ground, and as the Lanc got lower the wingtips got ever closer to crushing the farmer's garage and existing tool shed, over both of which they extended.

Therefore, when the farmer was approached by Found Brothers to see if he was interested in selling the Lancaster, he was quite keen to take up the offer – at the same time as getting some cash he would also save his outbuildings! The bomber was dismantled and the centre section sent to de Havilland.

Due to the strict requirements for interchangeability laid down for the production of the Lancaster Xs, KB895's centre section was fitted to the serviceable parts of FM213 with relative ease. This made the airframe effectively a hybrid of FM213 and KB895.

Repairs to the Lanc were completed in August 1953 and, after a flight test, on the 21st it finally arrived for service with 405 Sqn at Greenwood. The former bomber was soon at work in a rescue role, as the next day Lancaster 10MR KB999 was reported missing north of Churchill, Manitoba: 405 Squadron's Lancasters were sent to search for the missing crew on 23 August, with FM213 being part of the deployment.

Over the following days FM213 carried out several lengthy search patterns, including one of nearly 11½ hours. On 29 August the crew were all found alive by an SAR Douglas Dakota. Cigarettes and chocolates were then dropped to them out of the flare chute of FM213, before the Lanc returned to Greenwood on 1 September after its successful baptism into service.

FM213 did, however, spend the majority of its service life with 107 Rescue Unit at Torbay, Newfoundland. While with this unit the Lanc was coded CX-213. Its duties were varied, with the unit's Lancs being on 24-hour standby. Search and rescue was one primary role, which would often see the Lancaster looking for lost hunters and fishermen, cars in snowdrifts and fishing boats. The Lanc was also used to escort inbound aircraft flying over the North Atlantic towards Newfoundland with an engine shut-down, and additionally it acted as an escort to Royal flights passing through 107's operational area.

Notably, FM213 arrived at Prestwick, Scotland, on a number of occasions during 'Duckbutt' operations. These sorties would see the Lancs used to assist the ferrying of various

RCAF aircraft, such as Avro Canada CF-100 Canucks, across the Atlantic.

Lancasters would not only serve as search and rescue aircraft during 'Duckbutts', they would also be used as mobile homing beacons on which the transiting aircraft could get a fix. The Lanc would get into position at around the halfway point of the planned flight path and then begin to fly in a racetrack pattern at right angles to the ferrying aircraft's direction. This would normally be performed at a height of around 8,000 to 10,000ft.

The radio operator then broadcast a continuous signal on the relevant frequency and Morse code designator. Once the ferrying aircraft had passed the Lanc, it would follow them on to the next base. A Lancaster could be sent to a position on any of the various legs of these ferry flights: Goose Bay, Labrador; Sondrestrom, Greenland; Keflavik, Iceland; and Prestwick, Scotland.

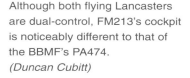

Although both flying Lancasters are dual-control, FM213's cockpit is noticeably different to that of the BBMF's PA474.
(Duncan Cubitt)

In 1959, requests were made to replace the Lancasters still in RCAF service. Among the concerns was the safety of the aircrews, a need to restrict the number of flying hours due to the age of the aircraft, a lack of spares and the difficulty of maintaining the Lancs to the standard required for their lengthy flights crossing vast areas of ocean.

But it took until 10 October 1963 for FM104 and FM213 to be authorised to be struck off strength. FM213 was finally retired from service on 6 November. It was first flown to Trenton, then placed into storage at Dunnville, having clocked up 4,392.3 hours of flying time.

Soon after this, the Hon. Paul Hellyer, Canadian Minister of National Defence, received a letter from the Goderich branch of the Royal Canadian Legion in Ontario. This letter was the result of Bill Clancy's campaigning during late 1963 to save wartime aircraft from being scrapped, and it received a speedy reply. In fact, fifty such applications had been made to request one of the remaining Canadian Lancs, and the one from Goderich was successful. A telex was sent out authorising the sale of FM213 in July 1964.

Once this was received, Bill's success resulted in his fellow Legion members forming a Lancaster Memorial Committee. A group then flew to Dunnville to formally receive their aircraft for the price of $1,300.

During the visit it was discovered that FM213 was in no condition to make a ferry flight to Goderich. About a week later Bill Clancy enquired if the situation had changed, only to be told that FM213's engines had been removed and installed into FM104 so that it could be flown to Toronto for display on the Harbourfront. On hearing this news, Bill called RCAF Headquarters in Ottawa and asked to speak to the Chief of the Air Staff. He was not impressed that this had occurred, and within days the engines were transported back from Downsview to Dunnville.

Civilian technicians then spent 400 hours bringing FM213 back up to flying condition. On 29 April 1964 the RCAF contacted the Lancaster's new owners informing them that it was now airworthy, that it was in place at Trenton receiving some final preparation, and that a crew would be provided to ferry the aircraft to Sky Harbour Airport.

An air show was organised to coincide with the arrival of the Lancaster, and an honour guard would also form part of the proceedings. On the day of its departure, FM213's maintenance crew fortunately made an early rise – one of the Lancaster's engines took two hours to get started! But once that hurdle had been overcome, the Lanc was reported to fly superbly and en route to Sky Harbour it carried out flypasts over several former wartime bases.

The Lancaster arrived at its destination one minute early, where it was officially received by retired AVM J.A. Sully on behalf of 109 Branch, Royal Canadian Legion, Goderich. This was part

Different to the Lancasters displayed on plinths elsewhere in Canada, FM213's airframe was left in a condition suitable for restoration to airworthy status because it was placed on three pylons – one at each of its jacking points. This is thought to be the Lancaster's dedication ceremony, held at Sky Harbour Airport on 15 September 1968.
(Courtesy Canadian Warplane Heritage Museum)

79

of a formal ceremony with a colour party and guard of honour, with the aircraft's logbook being handed over on a special RCAF tartan cushion.

FM213 was then left stored at Sky Harbour for a number of years until a permanent display site could be secured. Tours through the Lancaster became popular at the time, and fortunately it did not suffer from any vandalism. When sufficient funds had been raised to display the Lanc permanently, it was placed on three pylons at Sky Harbour. A dedication ceremony was held on 15 September 1968.

The fact that the Lanc was mounted on three pylons, one at each jacking point, was a crucial factor in it still being airworthy today. Most of the pylon-mounted Lancasters in Canada sat on a single large concrete plinth, which supported the aircraft in a place that made it necessary to cut the main spar.

As the years went by the aircraft's exposure to the elements, along with some depressingly inevitable vandalism, led to a deterioration in its appearance. Through various circumstances, the Lancaster's committee was whittled down to just three members, who between them could not keep up with the necessary repairs.

In 1975, CWHM member Bill Gregg was visiting friends in the Goderich area. After passing by the displayed Lanc Bill enquired about how it had arrived there and who owned it. Later, he and fellow CWHM member Murray Smith visited Sky Harbour to meet Bill Clancy. The man who had been instrumental in acquiring the Lancaster explained that he couldn't even get approval for the funding of a repaint, that the community had lost interest in it, and that weather and vandalism were taking their toll on the aircraft. It was evident that Bill Clancy didn't want to have to part company with the Lancaster, but also that he realised if something wasn't done soon there would be no alternative other than to consider a different future for the aircraft.

Bill and Murray then carried out an internal inspection. To their great delight, FM213's main spar was intact, and the Lanc remained in good condition inside, with the effects of vandalism being only external and minimal.

At the very next CWHM working session, the two men approached Dennis Bradley and Alan Ness, two of the CWHM's original directors and at the time the two senior executives. They were both keen on the idea of securing a Lancaster to bring up to airworthy status. The CWHM members then arranged to meet with the Legion's board of directors in Goderich. Initial negotiations were positive, but within the next few months opinions changed. However, the would-be purchasers persisted and within a year the Legion offered the Lancaster for sale for $10,000.

Things then took another turn, as the CWHM board did not want to pay that amount and the members taking a key role in its acquisition were not keen on paying cash. The deal was eventually settled through a bequest from the Sully Foundation – carrying the name of AVM Sully who had officiated at the aircraft's handover ceremony – with FM213 then being donated to the museum.

With all this set in place, the CWHM members arranged for FM213 to be lowered from its pylons. It was discovered that virtually no structural damage had been caused to the airframe when it was fitted onto the pylons, and as all three were at jacking points stress had also been kept to a minimum.

As no large crane was available, the plan was to attempt to lower the undercarriage, service the oleos, inflate the tyres and then cut the pylons. This all worked out fine, and FM213 was soon being towed across the road and back onto an airport hardstanding.

The ownership of FM213 transferred to the CWHM on 1 July 1977. It was agreed that the best way of moving the Lanc to its new home would be to take it apart and airlift it out of Sky Harbour by helicopter. A decision was made to ask the armed forces if they would be prepared to carry out the airlift as a training exercise. This was agreed upon in principle, provided that the aircraft's weight was reduced to a bare minimum – and so FM213 was extensively stripped.

First to make the trip to Mount Hope were the propellers, which were removed from the Lancaster during heavy snowfalls in the winter of 1977–8. Next to go were the ailerons, followed by the engines, one at a time. Then the rudders, elevators and various pieces of equipment from the Lancaster's interior were removed and transported to the museum. During the spring of 1979 the outer wings were removed from the airframe, a task which created a great deal of difficulty. But, once done, the fuselage was within weight limits for the helicopter lift.

Permission was obtained to use a Boeing CH-147 Chinook from 450 Sqn to lift the Lanc. The first attempt came in June 1979, but was aborted before the Lancaster left the ground as the load was thought to be still too heavy. It turned out that the problem had been the result of the three slings used being too short.

Another lift, this time using longer, 58ft slings, was attempted on 5 November 1979. The Chinook lifted the Lancaster off the ground, but there were still problems as the bomber's fuselage began to swing in the air even though an air drogue was trailing behind it for directional stability.

At all times the loadmaster had his thumb on a release button, in case the abnormal load presented a danger to the Chinook. Reportedly, this was almost pressed on more than one occasion during the transit; but for the most part the Lancaster straightened up in flight and after 1 hour 40 minutes was safely deposited on the ground at Hamilton. The fuselage joined the

other parts of the bomber, placed at the back of Hangar 4 awaiting restoration.

Because the CWHM was a charitable foundation with limited funds and voluntary members, the prospect of restoring such a large and complicated four-engined bomber was formidable. Although some cleaning and dismantling took place soon after its arrival, the Lancaster sat largely untouched for several years.

The catalysts which got the project going came in early 1983. First the museum was awarded a substantial grant from the Federal Government; then aircraft engineer Norm Etheridge agreed to lead and train the team of apprentices that would restore it.

Norm was already familiar with the CWHM. He was the engineer who had inspected the its first aircraft, a Fairey Firefly acquired in 1972, and certified that it was in airworthy condition. Norm's experience in the Royal Navy had

FM213 coming in to land after its successful airlift to Hamilton by a Chinook on 5 November 1979. A first attempt was made in June 1979, but was aborted before the Lancaster left the ground, as the three supporting slings used were too short. In this photo the longer 58ft slings are evident.
(Courtesy Canadian Warplane Heritage Museum)

convinced the Department of Transport that he was qualified to do this.

Work on the Lanc began on 24 March 1983. From the outset Norm had stated to the CWHM management that the aircraft would have to be restored his way in order that it would be acceptable to the Department of Transport and meet his licence requirements. To bolster the team of four apprentices, some of the museum volunteers who had been involved with the aircraft at an earlier stage came forward offering help. As most had no experience of aircraft maintenance, Norm would direct them to other areas where they could assist, such as cleaning.

Tasks required to restore the fuselage included stripping the paint inside and out, removing the postwar radar dome and plating over the hole, taking out the two observation windows just in front of the tail and covering over the apertures. Another complicated task at this time was the replacement of the wooden rear part of the canopy frame, the astrodome and the bomb aimer's window in the nose.

Progress continued apace, and during April and May 1985 all the work on the wings, trailing edges and flaps came together as by then all these components had been fitted back onto the Lancaster. As the engine mounts went onto the wings, which soon also boasted their wingtips back in place, FM213 was really beginning to take shape. Its restoration to represent the configuration of a wartime bomber was also becoming noticeable at this time, as the front turret was partially completed.

The Lanc was given an airing in this condition at the 1985 Hamilton Air Show. FM213 formed the most appropriate centrepiece for a display of its Lancaster Support Club, which had been formed in late 1984.

As the restorations of the turrets neared completion, the problem of 'arming' them needed careful consideration. Six Browning 0.303in and two 0.5in machine guns would be needed, and the answer was to obtain genuine examples as patterns and make dummy guns to represent the Lancaster's originals.

On their arrival at Mount Hope, it soon became evident that FM213's engines were all unserviceable – piston rings had even rusted onto cylinder walls. To get the Lancaster flying again would require a complete set of four Packard Merlin 224s overhauled to zero-timed condition.

The search for these had started before the restoration had begun. Two time-expired engines in excellent condition were acquired still in their protective cases, and the CWHM also negotiated the procurement of the four engines from Lancaster X KB889 at Oshawa, Ontario (now at the Imperial War Museum Duxford, Cambridgeshire).

A favourable deal was then struck to have four engines plus a spare overhauled by a company in Minneapolis, Minnesota. These were shipped out in 1983, and while they were away attention in Canada turned to associated items such as the engine bearers.

Over the next few years various companies came on board and assisted the project significantly by offering to overhaul, test and have approved other components such as instruments, electric starters, generators, air compressors, fuel pumps, hydraulic pumps and actuators. This all significantly helped to keep the project within the strict budget.

The first of the Merlins to be completed was ground-tested on 14 April 1986. After a successful outcome, this arrived at the CWHM the following month. It was fitted to the aircraft in the No. 3 position complete with a temporarily fitted propeller in time for that year's Hamilton Air Show in June. After the show the propeller was removed and the museum's engineers set to fitting all the coolant and oil lines plus the throttle, mixture and pitch control-system cables and chains.

No. 2 engine was tested on 19 January 1987 and arrived in February. It was fitted during April. For that year's air show both engines were fitted with propellers, and the outboard engine positions were temporarily mounted with some of the cowlings in place.

However, a problem with completing the remaining two engines had appeared during that spring. For all the engines sent for overhaul, there was a shortage of serviceable major components such as cylinder banks and cylinder heads. This was resolved after the CWHM's problem was highlighted to the Canadian Armed Forces base at Greenwood, which had Lancaster X KB839 on display. Through the generosity of the base commander, an agreement was reached whereby the CWHM could remove all the engine components they desired as long as externally the aircraft looked complete, with propellers and exhaust stacks visible. Members of FM213's restoration team spent ten days at Greenwood during May removing the engines. KB839 had propellers and exhaust stacks fitted back into place convincingly to appear as though nothing was missing inside the cowlings, while four engines and a number of large boxes filled with Lancaster components headed for Hamilton. The Merlins were firstly inspected by the museum's engine crew, then sent to Minneapolis, bringing the total number of engines dispatched to more than twenty.

The batch of engines from KB839 ideally solved the problem. FM213's third overhauled engine was tested on 11 August. It arrived the following month and was fitted to the No. 4 position (starboard outer). Then, on 5 February 1988, the fourth engine arrived at the museum. The following month this was put into place in the No. 1 position (port outer). The focus then turned towards installing all the equipment and controls with a view to the exciting prospect of being able to carry out ground test runs.

It was decided that on completion of the project the Lancaster would be painted to represent KB726, a Lancaster X which served on 419 Sqn during the war (more of which later). It was therefore quite fitting that the former pilot of the original KB726, Art de Breyne, provided a significant input towards the restoration. Art arranged for all forty-eight of the exhaust stubs to be repaired, or, where their condition due to damage or corrosion was too poor to consider repair, to be remade. This work was done by a specialist stainless-steel pipe-component company which Art had once owned.

The propellers were all overhauled by another specialist company. They were found to be in relatively good condition and were brought up to specification at no cost to the museum. The same company also balanced the spinners.

Another problem which had arisen early on in the project was that FM213 had arrived at the CWHM minus all of its fire bottles. A company in Montreal had offered to assist with fitting a modern fire-extinguisher system to the Lanc, but it lacked the eight bottles that were needed.

This problem was solved in a somewhat unfortunate manner. On arriving at Hamilton in poor visibility on 19 June 1986, ready for the Hamilton Air Show on the 21st, RAF Handley Page Victor K.2 XL191 was damaged beyond repair after bouncing on landing and flying into the ground – fortunately, all on board were OK. The Victor was broken up following the accident, and as all its fire bottles had been activated they were thrown aside. The seven bottles that were suitable for use on the Lanc were acquired by the museum and sent away for refurbishment, with an eighth bottle to make up the full complement being supplied by the Montreal company.

FM213's undercarriage caused particular problems. It was discovered that it was not going to be possible to repair the oleos to the necessary standard, and also that the Lancaster's tyres were

Below the pilot's window on both sides of the forward fuselage 'KB726' wears this nose art featuring the Victoria Cross, Andrew Mynarski's name and the date of the actions that won the brave airman his VC.

not going to be of any use for an airworthy aircraft. The tyres were already twenty years over their life; there were no more Lancaster tyres available and even the moulds were no longer around – so the idea of having more made was rejected.

Attention turned to looking at the possibility of using Avro Lincoln tyres. This would also require Lincoln oleo legs, brakes and wheel assemblies. It was then noted that suitable tyres were fitted to the Avro Shackleton, which at the time had just had its life extended by the RAF. As a result of this, the CWHM were able to order six sets of brand new Shackleton tyres from the manufacturers in the UK.

With ample tyres secured, the hunt then turned towards the acquisition of some Lincoln wheel sets. It turned out that a set was available for purchase in the UK. This equipment was inspected and assessed as being in good-enough condition for refurbishment, so arrangements were made to move it all to RAF Brize Norton in Oxfordshire, from where it could be picked up by the next available visiting Canadian Armed Forces Lockheed C-130 Hercules. This happened without incident, and the wheel sets were delivered to Trenton, from where they were taken to Hamilton by road. The oleos were sent away for inspection, and although a number of areas were found which would need repairs or replacement components, the result was that they were fit to be used on the Lanc.

In the summer of 1988, FM213 was repainted in its wartime scheme representing Lancaster X KB726 VR-A. The original KB726 was the aircraft in which Plt Off Andrew Mynarski won

Inside the rear fuselage of FM213 is this display board, which includes a picture of Andrew Mynarski.

Prior to a busy day's flying, FM213 is fuelled up with 100LL on the museum ramp at Hamilton.

his posthumous Victoria Cross on 12/13 June 1944. His Lanc had been badly shot up and set on fire by a Ju 88 night-fighter near the target at Cambrai. Mynarski suffered severe burns trying to save the rear gunner, Pat Brophy, who was trapped in his burning turret. By a twist of fate, the gunner survived the ordeal when the Lanc finally crashed and exploded, but Mynarski, who had baled out, died of his burns soon afterwards.

Two of KB726's surviving crew were captured and interned in prisoner-of-war camps, but four evaded the Germans. When he was repatriated after the war, Mynarski's actions were reported to a higher authority by Pat Brophy. So on 11 October 1946, Andrew Mynarski was awarded a posthumous Victoria Cross. Buried in France, Mynarski was later remembered in several ways. A high school in Winnipeg was renamed after him, as was a housing development in Alberta, and a group of lakes in northern Manitoba were

collectively named the Mynarski Lakes. An annually presented RCAF award was also called the Mynarski Trophy, and then FM213 became the Mynarski Memorial Lancaster, flying on in memory of one of Canada's brave young airmen who never returned across the Atlantic to see his family and homeland again.

It was planned that FM213's first post-restoration engine runs would be carried out on 9 August. However, this had to be cancelled due to a weather forecast which had predicted thunderstorms. This notwithstanding, still sitting on its Lancaster undercarriage to keep it mobile, the bomber was fuelled up for the first time in twenty-four years, and no leaks were found. Then, at 1115hrs on 10 August, the No. 4 engine was fired up, and with the characteristic puff of blue smoke it burst into life. It was run for five minutes before developing a small fuel leak at the carburettor. Next was the No. 1 engine, which

Just to see the Lancaster start up and taxi out is a thrilling experience, and one which always attracts a large crowd of spectators with their cameras at the ready.

was fired up just after 1120hrs. This was run for two minutes before it developed a fuel leak at the supercharger nozzle. Following rectification to cure the leak, the No. 4 was then restarted and left to run for fifteen minutes. No. 3 was turned over next, but only ran for two minutes until a hydraulic line blew. The engineers worked on the necessary areas and at 1530hrs all four engines were running at the same time. They were left idling for around thirty minutes, and all temperatures and pressures were reading satisfactorily within limits. Other minor snags occurred on subsequent ground runs, and the correction of these plus the adjustment of various controls went on for some time to get everything ticking over just right.

While this was going on, the need for the Lincoln undercarriage to be ready became a primary concern, as the plan was for the Lancaster to make its inaugural flight on 24 September. On 20 August the new main gear assemblies were ready. FM213 was put on jacks so that the undercarriage could be swapped and then put through a series of rigorous retraction tests – all this meaning that the ground-run test schedule was interrupted. A formal inspection was carried out on 6 September, and numerous snags were discovered, though all were only minor in nature.

August that year also saw the fitting of the radio equipment into the Lanc. This would all need to be suitable for navigation on fairly long-

Here, one of the oleos is being disassembled for cleaning and inspection during February 2005. New seals will be installed ready for the new season. From left to right: Keith Childs, Jim Buckel and Garth Stratham.
(Randy Straughan)

distance trips, and as such modern devices were essential. The CWHM was gifted a complete King Golden Crown III Series avionics package. The various bits of communication and navigational equipment supplied required five different types of aerials to be fitted on the fuselage.

With everything complete and good to go, and by then registered as C-GVRA, the first flight was planned for 10 September. But, during the pre-flight run-ups, a mag-drop problem occurred on one of the engines. To make the day at least productive, high-speed 'taxi runs' were carried out with the tail in the air to see how the Lanc handled. The mag-drop problem was cured by a spark-plug change.

The following day, 11 September 1988, was to witness the occasion everyone had worked so hard for. The crew consisted of former OC BBMF Sqn Ldr Tony Banfield as captain, co-pilot Bob Hill, and flight engineers Norm Etheridge and Tim Mols. At 1325hrs FM213 took to the air in the guise of KB726.

Various handling, flying-characteristic and system checks were carried out during the hour-long maiden test flight. On being lowered the undercarriage was found to be very slow extending and locking, suggesting air in the hydraulics. However, 'KB726' landed safely at 1425hrs.

A second test flight was carried out three days later. During this sortie, a serious problem occurred when an undercarriage retraction actuator line fractured. The situation was worsened when a progressive failure of the electrical system arose as the result of a faulty contact in one of the regulators. The fractured line led to a loss of hydraulic fluid, which then allowed air into the system that caused both hydraulic pumps to seize. The emergency undercarriage deployment system was activated and worked perfectly. FM213 landed safely after a flight of 1.35 hours.

Yet another parts problem had now arisen, as the Lancaster needed replacement hydraulic pumps. The situation was given added pressure as the planned date for the inaugural flight was fast approaching. The only suitable pumps available in Canada were those fitted to KB944 at the Canada Aviation Museum in Ottawa. Fortunately, these were procured and at the same time all the hydraulic lines to the undercarriage, flaps and bomb-bay doors were replaced. The hydraulic system was then refilled and bled to ensure there was no air in it.

With all the faults cured, on 23 September, the day before the inaugural flight, three progressively longer test trips were flown by various crews. The Lancaster was ready for its big day just in the nick of time!

Early-morning preparations for flight include pre-oiling the engines, the primary reason being to supply oil to the camshafts prior to starting; Merlins have a history of metal flaking off the cam lobes. The procedure also supplies oil to the crankshaft main bearings and rod bearings. To carry out this task the crew connect a small auxiliary pump directly to the oil-pressure regulator, and two gallons of oil are then pumped into the engine. The first gallon is pumped with the engine at rest. During pumping of the second gallon the engine is cranked two to three times using the starter motor, counting six blades each time. Cranking the engine allows the oil to be distributed thoroughly about the camshaft.

Some of the Lancaster crew take time out from their busy schedule for a group portrait! The museum's Chief Engineer, Duane Freeman, is second from right on the front row.

A civilian aircraft needs a civilian registration – even if it's a Lancaster.

Most of the original Mynarski crew and their families were there to witness the occasion, and they were joined by Andrew Mynarski's sister. Amid much media coverage, and with many high-profile dignitaries among the guests, the ceremonies began at 1400hr. The original fire axe from KB726, which Plt Off Andrew Mynarski had used to try to help Pat Brophy escape, was presented to the Lancaster's pilots to be flown on board for this occasion.

The air show began at 1420hrs, then at 1530hrs the much anticipated take-off of 'KB726' arrived. After a few solo flypasts, the Lanc was joined by the CWHM's Hawker Hurricane and a privately owned Supermarine Spitfire for a flypast à la BBMF. The 20,000 spectators there to witness the occasion were thrilled.

Ever since, 'KB726' has been the museum's flagship and has graced the skies of North America on a very regular basis. In the years soon after its completion, the Lancaster appeared at air shows not only in Canada but also in the US. It has visited every Canadian province except Newfoundland, and has at least flown over, if not visited, no less than nineteen US states, venturing as far south as Galveston, Texas.

In recent years, though, this has changed and nowadays the Lancaster tends to stay mostly closer to home – within about a 100-mile radius – being flown primarily for the regular members' flights. As the anniversaries of Second World War-related events dwindled during the latter part of the last century, the museum was at the same time made aware that maintenance costs were going nowhere but up. Also, in the post-9/11 world fewer air shows meant fewer hours, and fewer hours divided into much higher costs means wildly escalating hourly rates.

The law in Canada mandates that the CWHM cannot operate with capital debt, i.e. operating revenue must cover costs. What many air show organisers cannot accommodate, considering North American geography, is that they have to pay all of the transit costs as well as the flying time at their event. An example of this is for a venue on the west coast, which would require a 10-plus hour transit out and the same back, for air show flying time that will be well under an hour.

Whenever the museum receives an invitation, the arithmetic is carried out and the planning team will arrive at a comparison of the costs versus revenue by going to the show compared to staying at home. One of the absolutes is that if the Lancaster goes away the museum revenues plunge during its absence. Increasingly nowadays it seems that the museum's financial welfare is often better served by the Lanc staying at home.

The Canadian Warplane Heritage Museum is often referred to as 'Canada's Flying Museum'. This term is not given to it lightly, as many of the museum's fleet of aircraft are maintained in airworthy trim. So, not only are visitors able to go to the museum to see its exhibits, the aircraft can also be taken out to the people.

As well as the Lanc, the museum's resident airworthy aircraft include: Beech C-45 Expeditor '143' (C-GZCE); Boeing Stearman PT-17 Kaydet FK107 (C-FAIU); Consolidated PBY-5A Canso A '9754' (C-FPQL); DHC Chipmunk 2 18041 (C-FBXK); Douglas DC-3 Dakota 'KN456'/'KN563' (C-GDAK); Fairchild PT-26 Cornell '163' (C-FYYY); Fairey Firefly AS.5 'VH142' (C-GBDG); North American B-25J Mitchell III 45-8883 (C-GCWM); and North American Harvard IV 20213 (C-FUUU). A most impressive mix of types to see flying, by anyone's standards!

Along with all the other airworthy aircraft, the CWHM operates FM213 with the utmost care and to strict guidelines laid down by Transport Canada (the Canadian equivalent of the UK's CAA). Recent years have seen the Lanc carry out as many as thirty-five flights a year. This sees it log in the region of over forty hours in the air. The bomber's flying season begins in April or May, and its last flight of the year is for Remembrance Day on 11 November. FM213 then goes in for its scheduled winter maintenance programme.

Obviously, a large and complicated aircraft such as a Lancaster requires an incredible amount of behind-the-scenes logistics and a great deal of money to keep it airworthy. A significant

The Canadian Warplane Heritage Museum's 'KB726' is the world's only civilian-operated airworthy Lancaster.
(Duncan Cubitt)

percentage of the CWHM's income goes towards keeping its aircraft flying. To this end, the CWHM has a team of three full-time professional engineers, headed by Chief Engineer Duane Freeman who oversees every maintenance and restoration task carried out. The museum then relies on the efforts of its large volunteer force to carry out the bulk of the work.

It wears the 419 'Moose' Sqn codes VR-A to represent KB726 in honour of Plt Off Andrew Mynarski. Note also the representative Martin 250CE mid-upper turret.

William (Bill) Kondra DFM was an NCO bomb aimer with 100 Sqn at Waltham, Grimsby, during the Second World War. Eleven of Bill's thirty ops were to Berlin, and he was awarded a non-immediate DFM for a difficult tour of operations. On completion of his tour in January 1944, Bill was commissioned. After the war he re-enlisted in the RCAF and qualified as a Lancaster flight engineer – he went on to fly in FM213 from Greenwood. Bill thought he should not pass up the opportunity to join the CWHM as a member of the Lancaster crew and to take to the air in this aeroplane again. He is seen in the nose of FM213 reacquainting himself with the bomb aimer's panel just before his flight in June 2004.

This wartime crew photo was taken upon completion of Bill Kondra's tour in January 1944. Bill is pictured in the centre of the line-up.
(Courtesy Bill Kondra)

In total the museum's engineering volunteers number over fifty. The CWHM is a civilian 'approved maintenance organisation' governed by Transport Canada. They must work strictly within the approvals laid down – very few people have approvals for the types of aircraft worked on at the CWHM. Regular audits are carried out by qualified inspectors to ensure that the

compared with most other aircraft at the museum. On top of the scheduled work, the engineers have to deal with any 'snags' and running maintenance that may occur during the flying season.

The Lancaster team comprises a core group of about eighteen volunteers. These turn up on Wednesdays and Saturdays and, as mentioned, all

Photographed in late February 2005 is a newly delivered overhauled Merlin 224 for the No. 3 position of 'KB726'.
(Jeff Young)

engineers are working within their guidelines. The Lancaster never had a civilian type certificate, therefore the approvals and guidelines have been drafted by the CWHM and Transport Canada working together.

The Lancaster's maintenance programme is broken up into one- and three-year schedules, 50-hour and 100-hour inspections, known as 'A' and 'B' checks. FM213 is very labour-intensive

their work is reported to the museum's Chief Engineer. The group works to a strict protocol of inspections.

Major tasks carried out on the Lancaster over the winter of 2004–5 saw the replacement of its No. 3 (starboard inner) engine and a major inspection of the No. 4 engine (starboard outer), including the removal of the 'A' bank to replace gaskets and seals as it had been leaking oil.

To cure a persistent oil leak, No. 4 engine's 'A' bank was removed during February 2005 to have new gaskets and seals installed. Brian Jackland (left) and Graham Secord are seen preparing to reinstall the bank. *(Randy Straughan)*

A newly overhauled Packard Merlin 224 arrived at the museum on 19 February 2005, and the existing No. 3 was lifted off early the following month. The new engine was fitted into place during mid-March 2005 ready to be set up for the new flying season.

The Lancaster's volunteers come from a wide variety of backgrounds, everything from retired teachers to industrial engineers. There are four crew chiefs as part of the team. It is estimated that the volunteer workforce provides in the region of 4,000 man-hours each year on maintenance, and the aircrew around 500 hours in total on crewing the Lanc. That is why the job is not so much a hobby, more a vocation. This is the kind of commitment and team effort that has kept the aircraft flying all these years.

In Britain PA474 is operated by the RAF's Battle of Britain Memorial Flight, and, though there are some similarities between civilian and military methods, the procedures in place are generally very different. In common with the RAF operation, there is a very strict selection procedure for pilots on the Canadian Lanc. Much of this came down to a pilot's background, as the CWHM ideally wanted people with heavy multi-piston tail-dragger experience – but these aren't tremendously common. Once a pilot was selected, there was then a natural evolutionary scale of types flown: Chipmunk, Harvard, Beech 18, Dakota and finally Lancaster. The level of

Lancaster Crew Chief Randy Straughan cleans the inside of FM213's windscreen before a sortie. Randy became involved with the Lanc as his grandfather served as a wireless operator on Lancasters with 153 Sqn at Scampton from October 1944 to March 1945.

Training captain and check pilot on the CWHM Lancaster is Don Schofield, a former RCAF and Air Canada pilot.

training and currency then carried out is governed by the basic minimums which are imposed upon the CWHM by Transport Canada.

The Dakota is particularly important to the training programme, as it allows new pilots to become familiar with handling a multi-engine tail-wheel aircraft. In common with PA474, FM213 is landed with the 'wheel it on' approach rather than a 'three-pointer', and the 'Dak' helps the pilots to perfect this method. The whole set-up is centred around a 'safety first' policy, so the Dakota's part in ensuring that a would-be pilot is at home with that type of aircraft is crucial.

Presently, there are five Lancaster pilots. Don Schofield is the Training captain/Check Pilot, and has truly worked his way 'up the ranks'. Don is a former RCAF pilot who during his service career flew such types as the Chipmunk, Harvard, T-33, CF-100 Canuck and CF-101 Voodoo – ironically, he was almost posted onto Lancs! After his air force career Don went on to become an airline pilot with Air Canada, flying various types including the Boeing 747. Don's distinction at the end of his airline career was that he became the first pilot ever to be current on the Airbus A330/A340 and the Lancaster at the same time. One might think that there was no relationship until you realise that the Trent engine on the A330 and the Merlin share that finest of trademarks – Rolls-Royce. One of the traditions at Air Canada is to have an official portrait taken with your wife against your last steed, and Don's sure that his choice of VR-A as a backdrop raised a few eyebrows!

On top of all this experience, Don had a lot of time on the DHC-4A Caribou twin-piston transport, giving him a great pedigree for consideration as a pilot on the Lancaster.

During the 1980s Don found he had a good deal of spare time on his hands, and he knew that the restoration of FM213 was in progress at this point. He ended up turning up at the museum just to do something almost therapeutic – starting by scraping paint and washing and cleaning various parts while others took the aeroplane apart.

One of Don's Air Canada colleagues, Bob Hill, was nominated as the Chief Pilot designate. When the Lancaster's return to flight became a reality, thoughts turned to how it was going to be crewed. Bob asked Don if he wanted to become involved with this; if so, Bob would be happy to put Don's name forward. The rest, as they say, is history, as after two or three years as a co-pilot Don was checked out as a captain and has gone on to achieve around 500 hours on the Lanc.

Some words from Don sum up what his experience on the Lanc has taught him about how to handle the bomber: 'We fly the aircraft

Pilots Don Fisher (left) and Don Schofield take FM213 back towards Hamilton from Toronto, flying along the edge of Lake Ontario. On normal transit flights the Canadian Lanc cruises at 180 knots, with the Merlins set to run at 2,200rpm and +2 boost.

With the pilots in their seats, Crew Chief Jeff Young begins his busy schedule of checks to prepare the Lancaster for flight. Jeff originates from Scotland and has two mechanical loves in his life: the Lanc and his 'wee MG'!

FM213 has been known to operate from grass runways, such as here at the Wings of Eagles Air Show, Geneseo, New York, on 19 August 1990.
(Duncan Cubitt)

very conservatively. There is no latitude with the Lancaster to be the slightest bit aggressive. You have to anticipate what the aircraft is going to do in certain aspects of its operation. It's an aircraft with a great deal of inertia so you have to be on the ball at all times when you are airborne.'

Don has worked out a successful training routine for the type. He gives the pilots numerous trips of an hour each to get them up to type rating. To carry crew passengers on board, the pilots must have carried out four landings within the previous month. They are all professional pilots, and an accurate record is

kept of all their hours on the Lanc. The other four pilots are: Don Fisher (retired Air Canada on Boeing 747s); Richard Pulley (retired Air Canada 747); Sten Palbom (current Air Canada, on the Airbus A320); and Gary Schroeder (current corporate pilot).

Whereas the BBMF crews wear standard RAF-issue flying helmets and oxygen masks, the CWHM pilots wear airline-type headsets. While the latter are perhaps more comfortable to wear, they are not really designed to withstand the high level of noise that reverberates around the inside of a Lancaster in flight.

The CWHM Lancaster's engine start sequence also differs from that used by BBMF. For FM213 the sequence goes No. 4, 3, 2 then 1. With PA474 the start-up sequence goes No. 3, 4, 2 then 1. This is because the generators and compressors are configured differently on the Canadian Lanc. Apart from the sequence, though, the start-up procedure is similar to that of PA474.

Since its entry into regular service FM213 has rarely gone unserviceable. Over the years the crews have had to carry out only two or three engine shut-downs. One of these occurred a number of years ago at Greenwood, Nova Scotia, and required the change of one of the engine 'banks'. There was another similar 'bank' change in Calgary a few years later. The challenge in carrying these out far away from the Lancaster's home base was that the engine was still on the wing, and not on a maintenance stand at floor level. Taking all the spares and tools back and forth obviously caused great problems due to the distance away from home.

Enough fuel is now kept on board at all times so that should a problem occur requiring an in-flight shut-down, the crew can recover to home base rather than landing at the show venue and possibly marooning the aircraft there for a long time while repairs are made as highlighted in the cases above. The local rules are that with a twin-engined aeroplane if you shut an engine down it is an automatic emergency – the generic is land it at the nearest suitable airport. With a four-engined aeroplane, unless it is something as serious as a fire, it's just a case of a precautionary

C-GVRA heads toward Toronto with Don Fisher at the controls.

One of those pictures that simply doesn't seem real – the view over FM213's starboard wing during a flypast just off Toronto's Harbourfront. Defining the Toronto skyline at just over 1,815ft high, the CN Tower is probably Canada's most recognisable and celebrated icon. Toronto is one of the destinations used for the CWHM bomber crew members' flights.

shut-down and head home. If the Lancaster has to land somewhere else with a problem, its unique nature makes it something of a 'whale out of water'.

While out in Canada to fly FM213, Tony Banfield described the BBMF display sequence to the CWHM pilots. A similar routine was worked out for FM213, until the fire in the CWHM's old hangar on 15 February 1993, which saw the disastrous loss of the museum's Hawker Hurricane XII 'P3069' (C-GCWH) and privately owned Supermarine Spitfire IX MK297 (NX9BL). Since the fire the Lanc has essentially been a solo act.

FM213's display sequence is very similar to the BBMF's, as there is really not that much more that can be done to demonstrate the type. The

only thing that the CWHM developed which was a little bit different at the time was that the pilots started carrying out a topside pass. Coming in from one end of the crowd line, some bank is put on so that the aircraft flies along the crowd line in an arcing turn, offering the spectators splendid views of its topsides and consequently great photo opportunities. So the CWHM Lancaster's display roughly comprises topside pass, bottom-side pass, bomb doors open, gear and flaps down. The display lasts for a maximum of about twelve minutes – any more would start to see the routine repeating itself. Nowadays the Lancaster carries out relatively few air show displays, though.

FM213 has flown in large formations at air shows, too, and once it flew with the Canadian

Snowbirds display team. But, again, as the years have passed fewer opportunities to do this have arisen.

If the aircraft is going to go away to an air show, the pilots will look at the geography of the airport and the display line. Then, using those basic manoeuvres previously listed, they'll go out and take a couple of practices.

The pilots are not confined by needing to have air show endorsements; nor are they restricted by needing to have an approved set routine. This is basically left up to the aircraft captain and the geography of the show. Furthermore, they don't need a display authorisation as their UK counterparts would.

Another point of interest is that FM213 has been known to operate from grass runways, such as during its appearance at the Wings of Eagles Air Show, Geneseo, New York state, in August 1990. However, this was always the exception rather than the norm.

FM213 sits within the 'four-engined heavy' bracket of Transport Canada's categorisation process. And though generally North American ATC personnel also refer to it as a 'heavy', the term is rather misleading – certainly the aircraft is big, but it's not that heavy! However, because of this categorisation some show organisers aren't prepared to let the Lancaster do anything other than fly a racetrack pattern up and down the runway.

The only recent development concerning how to fly the Lancaster is a change in transiting procedure. When transiting in previous years the pilots used to fly instrument flight rules (IFR). Some of them remember flying the bomber in very poor visibility, and finding it to be a very capable aeroplane in such conditions. But a few years ago the Federal authorities noted very pointedly to the CWHM that warbirds don't always fit into the exact chapter and verse of current regulations.

FM213 was always being flown as two-pilot IFR. It was highlighted that the aircraft doesn't have two independent sets of flight instruments, it doesn't have a dual-pitot system, and it lacks various other necessary requirements. So, although basically it didn't change the aircraft's certification, as a matter of policy the pilots have restricted themselves to flying visual meteorological conditions (VMC) and under visual flight rules (VFR). As the Lancaster hasn't needed to

Toronto's CN Tower is the world's tallest tower and dominates the city's skyline. The white building noticeable at the foot of the CN Tower is the SkyDome, the impressive ballpark home of the Toronto Blue Jays baseball team.

carry out many major transits since then, this change hasn't caused many problems.

Crosswind limitations imposed on FM213 are basically similar to the BBMF's PA474. That means there is a maximum limit of 15 knots. Also identical to PA474's limitations are the maximum 'g' loadings imposed on the Canadian Lanc: these are a maximum of 1.5g, and a 'never exceed' of 1.8g.

FM213's pilot's operating handbook has been fine-tuned in house. The museum was in possession of all sorts of different Lancaster manuals, including the last ones that were in use when the type was operated by the RCAF. The pilots then rewrote the entire book to apply directly to that specific aeroplane as it was rebuilt. The book uses all the numbers from all these different sources that best applied to FM213 because the aircraft is unique. An ongoing process of amendment is part of keeping the manual appropriately in harmony with the Lancaster's characteristics.

The idea was that, in order for the government to approve it, everything had to be seen, including the manual. FM213's manual is thin, but it's quite accurate. It doesn't contain piles of charts and graphs for performance procedures.

With most of the pilots being former and current airline captains, it's hardly surprising that a series of airline-type checklists have been developed. These are carried out with the standard challenge-and-response procedure, and are rigidly adhered to.

Of particular note, FM213's fuel-dump system has been removed. Basically, if the system was fitted in the aeroplane it had to be up and running and serviceable. The authorities would then have required the CWHM to empty two tanks of fuel once a year, fill the tanks with distilled water, activate the dump system and dump the water on the floor to prove that it works.

FM213 has a maximum landing weight of 53,000lb, so the museum asked whether, if the crew limit the take-off weight to the maximum landing weight, they would be allowed to remove the fuel-dump system. The reply was positive. As a result, the Lancaster is never loaded beyond 53,000lb. By doing this, FM213 can take off and, even if it was to lose an engine soon afterwards, it can return straight away and land. This is a good example of how the CWHM has tried to keep everything as mechanically simple, and reliable, as possible.

When FM213 was acquired it was still in its MR/MP fit; it had LF, MF, HF, VHF and UHF radios, three radar sets, a number of generators – and more! The restoration team cleaned everything out. All that was put back in, or has been additionally fitted, were the pieces of equipment which were particular to the bomber version. So much equipment was removed that around 800lb of ballast needed to be placed in the aircraft's tail in order to keep its centre of gravity where it should be.

If you look inside FM213 and compare it to a fully fitted bomber it is comparatively empty. This has sometimes come as something of a disappointment to some of the purists. Also, one of the very first things some people notice is the fact that the top turret is apparently 'wrong'. While it may be 'incorrect' for the Lancaster it is painted to represent, later batches of Lancaster Xs were indeed fitted with the Martin turret and these examples had their turret apertures positioned further forward.

CWHM initially asked the Federal authorities if FM213 could be modified back into original Lancaster X form. But if you start cutting holes in aeroplanes it obviously raises concerns, so the idea was stopped before it even got started.

Another concession is the aircraft's paintwork, as criticism has been levelled at the Lanc to the effect that wartime bombers didn't have this semi-satin finish. But judged by a different criterion the wartime paint was very poor in quality, with a flat finish, and came off at a great rate. FM213's choice of paint is for two reasons: it's both long-lasting and offers anti-corrosion protection.

As noted earlier, FM213 also has a few antennas sticking out that are not historically accurate. But, if the aim is to fly the Lancaster around in North America nowadays, you've got to have such devices. The instrument panel and a few other things 'up front' are not as they were in the war either, but again, if you want to fly in to a major international airport, you have got to have this equipment.

So, while technically it doesn't accurately represent the original aeroplane externally or internally, it becomes clear why when you take into account the compromises that have had to be made along the way. What is for sure is that the aviation-heritage scene became a better place with the addition of a Lancaster to the skies over Canada.

The Lancaster's turrets do not function and the aircraft is not allowed to carry anybody in its rear turret, because the strength of the Plexiglas is untested. The material currently fitted is certainly far better than it was back in the 1940s, but because it hasn't been proved scientifically it cannot be authorised. The only thing allowed to be carried in the bomb bay is a tow bar.

FM213 is crewed by two pilots, a crew chief and a crewman. Additionally, on members' flights four crew passengers can be carried on board. For the CWHM crew members who are carried as passengers, four seats have been fitted in the rear section of the fuselage. These were taken out of a Beechcraft King Air. When they were put in, the museum was asked for an engineering stress analysis of the floor of the Lanc – which is the roof of the bomb bay – versus the floor of a King Air! This was carried out by an aviation company

in Toronto. The specialists had to do a thirty-two page engineering study to get the necessary authorisation. When you consider that during wartime service Lancasters carried up to 22,000lb of bombs on that floor . . .

The net result of so much red tape is that, courtesy of this wonderful innovation, many CWHM members who have joined under the special category of 'Bomber Crew Membership' have enjoyed a flight in a Lancaster! For this, the CWHM asks for an appropriate membership fee and the applicant gets a one-year membership which includes all the privileges of a 'Sustaining Member', plus the opportunity to crew on the Lancaster during one flight.

The trips usually last for around an hour from chock to chock. Each flight will take the Lancaster to one of two famous local tourist destinations – either Toronto, dominated by the impressive CN Tower, or Niagara Falls.

Bomber crew member passengers sit on four seats towards the rear of the fuselage. Note the ear defenders!

Turning around towards Toronto Harbourfront for a low-level flypast.

The CN Tower is dubbed 'Canada's Wonder of the World'. Defining the Toronto skyline, it is probably Canada's most recognisable and celebrated icon. At just over 1,815ft high, it is the world's tallest building, and is an important telecommunications hub and the centre of tourism in Toronto. Around 2 million people visit the tower each year, which features a glass floor and observation deck at a height of 1,122ft and a café and indoor observation deck at 1,136ft.

Prominent at the foot of the western side of the CN Tower is the white SkyDome. Since June 1989 the SkyDome has been the home of the Toronto Blue Jays baseball team. The roof of this impressive stadium is retractable, covering one of the world's most advanced and luxurious ballparks.

At Niagara Falls you can only watch in awe as huge volumes of water flow over the Horseshoe Falls and drop away to form one of the most famous waterfalls in the world. For those who like statistics, this waterfall has a staggering 6 million ft^3 of water surging over the 2,200ft crest line every minute towards the 177ft drop. Just a short distance from the Horseshoe Falls, on the US side of the river, which forms a natural border between the two countries, are the American Falls.

Both Toronto and the Niagara Falls are great places to visit on the ground, and awesome to see from the air – but to see one of them from on board a Lancaster is enough to leave most people speechless!

The four members of the bomber crew will be given a thorough pre-flight briefing. First it is explained to them that they are members of the crew, and there is a brief outline of the aircraft's history. This briefing then explains to the crew everything from safety aspects to what they can expect from the flight. It goes on to outline emergency procedures and warn them that the aircraft is noisy inside during the flight – but that's what most crew members are there for! Obviously, to most people climbing around a Lancaster is a new and rather unfamiliar experience. A quote from pilot Don Fisher sums up the environment inside: 'It's not built for dancing in!'

Bomber-crew members come from all walks of life, and many are overseas members. During my visit to the museum to see the Lancaster in action a member present was one of the many who travel out from the UK for the experience.

As regards the link between our country and FM213, plans to fly the aircraft over to the UK have been looked into on a number of occasions. The latest of these offered the prospect of bringing the Canadian Lanc over to the UK during July 2005 to commemorate the

60th anniversary of the end of the Second World War. The plan was that the aircraft would then join BBMF's PA474 in a special flypast down The Mall in London and over Buckingham Palace. At the back of the formation, PA474 would have been able to carry out its latest poppy drop with FM213 in front of it. This visit could at last have given us the opportunity of seeing

FM213 taxies back in to the museum ramp at Hamilton after a sortie to Niagara Falls. Several members of the bomber's ground crew are always on hand to welcome it back, with tasks not only including marshalling it in but also taking the chocks out to secure the aircraft once it's parked.

The Canadian Lancaster's last flying engagement of the year takes place on Remembrance Day. In 2004 the Canadian Mint introduced a new quarter dollar for Remembrance Day, featuring a red poppy in the centre on the reverse side. On 11 November 2004 a batch of the special Canadian quarter dollars was flown on board FM213.
(Duncan Cubitt)

both the world's airworthy Lancasters flying together.

However, during late February 2005 the CWHM received a communication informing its staff that the MoD would not be able to raise the sponsorship required to bring the Lancaster over for the commemorative flypast. It also mentioned that nearly every avenue possible had been explored to try and make this happen, and that those who were trying to organise it felt personally saddened that they had not been able to succeed.

Obviously, this would have been a very serious undertaking on behalf of Canadian Warplane

Heritage and the decision to stay put was not one the museum took lightly. Those responsible would never even have considered it unless they were completely confident that the aircraft was capable of flying that distance.

The CWHM's Chairman of the Board, R.J. Franks, commented: 'I would like to thank the people of England and specifically Sqn Ldr Mike Buckland for putting in so much effort to try and make it happen.' And that was indeed a most appropriate gesture, as during the planning for this proposed venture everybody involved at the MoD, the RAF, the BBMF and several other organisations were forthcoming with generous offers of support for all areas of the logistics.

But one thing remains the same. FM213 continues to grace the skies over Canada in tribute to the country's association with this legendary bomber. Having seen for myself the work being done at the CWHM, I was left with a feeling of total admiration. Keeping this flying tribute airborne in civilian hands is a phenomenal task – and to be achieving it in such fine style shows that there is no shortage of passion and dedication being lavished on the Lanc from those who look after it. Long may their efforts be rewarded by the sight and sound of a Lancaster flying in Canada.

This Poppy Coin was flown on Lancaster CGVRA / FM213

Nov 11/2004
Flight Time 1.0
Air Time .8

CHAPTER 4

NX611 – Lincolnshire Aviation Heritage Centre

S urrounding the charm and passion that abounds at the Lincolnshire Aviation Heritage Centre at East Kirkby is flat agri-cultural land, looking tranquil and at peace. However, going back more than sixty years the scene would have been entirely different.

As dusk fell, the area around East Kirkby would have reverberated with the drones and roars of squadrons of Lancasters setting out on night operations over enemy territory. For many of the crews who headed off from East Kirkby, the Lincolnshire airfield would have been the last place they stood on their homeland soil – while the families of those lost on operations were left with just memories of a brave father, son, husband or brother.

It is in honour of the memory of these young aviators that the site of the former RAF East Kirkby has been rejuvenated to offer a sample of the atmosphere of a wartime Bomber Command station. The airfield was once home to 57 and 630 Sqns flying Avro Lancasters, in the heart of Bomber County; so it is appropriate that the star of the museum is Lancaster VII NX611 *Just Jane*, which regularly performs taxi runs around the site.

When towed outside, NX611 provides visitors with unrivalled opportunities for photography of a Lancaster.

The museum stands as a memorial dedicated to all Bomber Command personnel who never returned home from operations – and especially to Plt Off Christopher Panton. Christopher was a flight engineer on 433 Sqn RCAF based at Skipton-on-Swale, Yorkshire, flying the Handley Page Halifax. Aged just nineteen, on the night of 30/31 March 1944, he was killed during operations over Nuremburg. Christopher is buried at Dürnbach War Cemetery in Germany.

Two of Christopher's brothers, Fred Panton MBE and Harold Panton, were young teenagers still at school when their brother was lost on operations. As they grew older they became determined to do something to commemorate their much-loved brother's memory. Their first thought was to purchase a postwar Halifax, but as things worked out this plan never came to fruition. They continued to look elsewhere.

NX611 was built by Austin Motors at Longbridge, near Birmingham, in April 1945. This Lancaster was one of a batch of 150 B.VIIs earmarked for 'Tiger Force' and thus for service in the Far East. The bomber was fitted with 1,640hp Merlin 24s, which were especially suitable for use in the climate of its intended theatre of operations. However, the earlier-than-anticipated surrender of Japan meant that the bomber became surplus to requirements, so NX611 went into storage at 38 Maintenance Unit, Llandow, Glamorgan.

The aircraft remained there until April 1952, when it was purchased by the French Government. After being repainted in midnight blue and given the serial number WU-15, it was put to use on maritime patrol and air-sea rescue duties with the French Naval Air Arm (L'Aéronavale), operating out of bases in Brittany and Morocco as part of Escadrille de Servitude 55S. The 'WU' of NX611's new French serial number stood for 'Western Union', which was the agreement under which the Lancasters were sold to France.

In 1962 the Lancaster was overhauled and received a repaint in all-over white. During early November WU-15 was on its way to Noumeau, New Caledonia – a French island located about 1,000 miles east of Australia. Along with two other Lancs, NX622 and NX665 (now preserved respectively at Perth, Australia, and Austin, New Zealand), WU-15 was employed on a variety of tasks such as air-sea rescue and communication duties across a wide region of the Pacific operated by Escadrille de Servitude 9S (S for 'servitude' – general duties!). After just two years the three French Lancs were withdrawn from service.

Around this time the UK-based Historic Aircraft Preservation Society was looking to preserve a Lancaster. The French offered HAPS one of their retiring examples free of charge, and even offered to fly it to Australia for collection. And so it was that WU-15 arrived at Bankstown, near Sydney, New South Wales, in August 1964.

A painting of Fred and Harold's older brother, Plt Off Christopher Panton, who was lost on operations in a Halifax during the Second World War.
(Painting by G.E. Lea, used with the kind permission of Fred and Harold Panton)

Now: For the purposes of a BBC TV drama, NX611 carried out a number of fast taxi runs down the remains of East Kirkby's runway in February 2002. The object was to get the tail in the air to represent a take-off run – the assignment was quickly accomplished during the first day of trials!
(Duncan Cubitt)

Then: After being handed over by the French Navy, WU-15 (NX611) is seen at Bankstown near Sydney, in August 1964, to be made ready for its 12,000-mile journey home.
(Ken Ellis Collection)

The contributors who stepped forward to help WU-15 fly back to the UK were given tributes on the Lancaster's nose. The winged motif below the pilot's window is the unit badge of Escadrille de Servitude 9S.
(Ken Ellis Collection)

Prior to the mammoth flight home, the bomber would need an overhaul. To pay for this and the flight home a fund-raising campaign began. Assistance came from the Hawker Siddeley Group, the Royal Australian Air Force, the RAF, Shell and Qantas as well as many aviation enthusiasts.

WU-15 was overhauled, fitted with an extra fuel tank and test-flown. On 23 April 1965, by now given the British civil registration G-ASXX,

the bomber was moved to Mascot near Sydney ready for her much-publicised departure. The Lanc took off on the first leg of the 12,000-mile journey home two days later, on 25 April. The trip took nine days and totalled around seventy flying hours, with the aircraft landing back on UK territory at Biggin Hill, Kent, on 13 May to coincide with the opening of the airfield's 1965 International Air Fair.

Due to the expiry of permitted hours on one engine and propeller, G-ASXX then found itself grounded. The bomber was soon undergoing restoration, and this work took around two years to complete. It included overhauls and recertification of the engines, propellers and various other systems.

The bomber gained a coat of night-time camouflage paintwork, and added to this was its original RAF serial number, NX611. It was also given the 'squadron codes' HA-P in recognition of the owning group's initials, though this was also coincidentally the code of a 218 (Gold Coast) Sqn wartime Lancaster. The livery retained the 'Spirit of Surfers Paradise' logo on its port side, and NX611 later received the name *Guy Gibson* at a ceremony attended by the famous bomber pilot's father.

On 6 May 1967 NX611 took to the air again on its first test flight. A second was flown the following day, during which several problems were encountered. These included the failure of the No. 2 engine to feather; also, overspeeding at 3,200rpm with the fire-warning light activated,

WU-15's French Navy starboard fuselage roundel, joined by a kangaroo to highlight the Australian connection.
(Ken Ellis Collection)

111

With its British civil registration G-ASXX applied, NX611 was photographed from an RAF Coastal Command Avro Shackleton en route to the UK. *(Key Collection)*

the extinguisher was operated and the engine cut. Fortunately, pilot Flt Lt Neil Williams made a safe three-engined landing back at Biggin.

The third air test occurred on 9 May, and further problems occurred when there was a complete hydraulic failure after take-off. The wheels and flaps had to be blown down using the emergency air supply. After the Lanc had received remedial attention, the fourth test flight took place on 17 May. This was completely successful.

NX611's first public appearance was set for the weekend of 19/20 May, when the bomber was to travel to RAF Scampton to mark the 24th anniversary of the Dam Busters raid. On board were several former 617 Sqn wartime aircrew.

The Lanc made several other appearances, but without the required amount of sponsorship funding the expense of operating it, coupled with the fact that the RAF's PA474 began flying again around the same time, was to lead to NX611 being grounded again. Its last sponsored display took place at Filton, Bristol, on 15 June 1968.

HAPS was soon wound up, and Reflectaire Ltd took over its assets. On 30 March 1969 NX611 set off for its new home at Lavenham, Suffolk. While there the bomber lost its HA-P codes, which were replaced by GL-C lettering. This was to represent the initials of Gp Capt Leonard Cheshire VC DSO** DFC, one of ten wartime Lancaster pilots to be awarded the Victoria Cross. During a visit to Lavenham in November 1969, Leonard Cheshire was given the wonderful opportunity to taxi the Lanc.

On 7 February 1970 the aircraft was on the move again, this time to Hullavington, Wiltshire. On board for the trip was Richard Todd, who had become synonymous with Lancs due to his leading role as Guy Gibson in the 1955 film *The Dam Busters*. NX611's final flight took place on 26 June 1970, when it set off for Squire's Gate, Blackpool, Lancashire. On board this time was former 617 Sqn bomb aimer Ron Valentine, who was allowed to occupy his old crew position. Since its arrival back in the UK the Lanc had made fourteen flights.

With NX611 as the centrepiece, the plan was to establish an aviation museum at Blackpool and to keep the Lancaster in airworthy trim. However, the closest it came to this was during film work in February 1971 for ITV's *Family at War*, which saw the Lanc carry out fast taxi runs along the main runway – and this would be the last time the Lanc moved under its own power for almost twenty-five years. Financial difficulties were later experienced and a receiver was called in.

An auction of the museum's exhibits was held on 29 April 1972. Even though an engine was fired up in an attempt to impress potential buyers, few bidders came forward, and the Lanc failed to reach its reserve of £12,000. In the crowd at the auction was Fred Panton. Two days after the auction the Rt Hon. Lord Lilford made moves to purchase the aircraft privately. It was his desire that the Lancaster should remain in Britain.

However, though the Lanc had found a new owner, its future wasn't assured. A lengthy spell of exposure to salt air and a general lack of expert maintenance had taken their toll, and during the next winter a rapid deterioration of its overall condition was to follow, especially to the engines and propellers. The rent bill of £5 a day was mounting, and it became obvious that if something wasn't done the bomber could be facing the scrapyard.

NX611 touches down at Biggin Hill on 13 May 1965 after its epic 12,000-mile flight from Australia. *(Martin Collins Collection)*

Above: In November 1969, wartime Lancaster pilot and Victoria Cross winner Leonard Cheshire was given the opportunity to taxi a Lanc once more at Lavenham. Note that the bomber was by then painted in a more appropriate scheme and wore the name *Guy Gibson*. The bomb marks each had the names of various benefactors applied to them.
(Martin Collins)

Centre: Initially given the code HA-P after the initials of its owning group, NX611's code was later changed to GL-C, the initials of Gp Capt Geoffrey Leonard Cheshire VC, DSO**, DFC. The bomber is seen at Lavenham.
(Martin Collins)

Below: The view out over NX611's Nos 3 and 4 engines on its final flight from Hullavington to Squire's Gate on 26 June 1970. *(Martin Collins)*

Fred Panton, who had himself been interested in buying the aircraft, stepped in to persuade the RAF to preserve it. In January 1973 an engineering officer from RAF Scampton inspected the Lanc and concluded that it would be possible to dismantle the bomber, move it to the Lincolnshire base and with the goodwill of some enthusiastic volunteers restore it as a static exhibit. That April Lord Lilford visited Scampton and agreed to offer it on long-term loan.

Dismantling work began in August when RAF Scampton sent a team up to Blackpool. They were all on leave and billeted by the Army at a nearby camp, as there was a strictly limited budget. The first week of this work was carried out in awful wet weather, but even by the end of the first day the wheels and propellers had been removed and the aircraft lowered to an acceptable working height. It took the planned nine days to take NX611 apart, and six loads on board Queen Mary trailers to transport the Lanc to Scampton. Once there, a coherent plan was drawn up to restore and reassemble the bomber – again, all in spare time. A target date of April 1974 was set.

Following a thorough and meticulous restoration, a partially dismantled NX611 was moved for positioning at the main gate on 10 April 1974. Final reassembly began the following day, and the difficult task of positioning the Lanc was completed on the 25th, when the aircraft was finally lowered onto the concrete-and-steel supports that had been constructed for the axles.

Carrying the Scampton Station Flight code YF-C, NX611 took up the gate-guard duties at RAF Scampton, which had previously been carried out by R5868 before it left for the RAF Museum at Hendon. Postwar, the YF-C code is reported to have been applied to Guy Gibson's Lancaster B.III (Special) ED932, which he flew on the famous Dams raid. The reason for the bomber coming out of storage is that three of the specially modified Lancs were resurrected for Operation Guzzle, which was charged with disposing of more than forty surplus Upkeep mines.

This occurred in late August/September 1946, at a time when there were no squadrons at Scampton, only an MU preparing Avro Lincolns for squadron service. My first knowledge of Operation Guzzle came after I had written an article on the Dam Busters and a former 101 Sqn navigator wrote to me detailing his involvement. It transpired that a 101 Sqn crew, together with a crew from 617 Sqn, were attached to Scampton for the operation. The purpose of the exercise was to dispose of the Upkeeps in the deep Atlantic.

ED932, initially with no squadron markings (but just discernible on arrival was AJ-L so at sometime the original AJ-G had been re-lettered), was joined by ED906 which at the time was painted as AJ-G, plus a third aircraft that the navigator had not flown, for which reason he had kept no record of its identity.

The bombs were reported to be in a rather poor state according to the armourers (explosive crystallising, for example) and the course required a considerable amount of map-reading over the UK as the crews were understandably required to steer clear of any habitation en route. The loading of the bombs initially caused some amusement, because the weapon was unknown to the armourers and the aircrew 'disappeared at double time' on several occasions.

The route took the Lancs out over the west of Scotland, and the dropping zone was a fairly large area centred on 56.00N 12.00W. The bombs were not to be dropped from below 10,000ft. During the time frame the weather offered an Atlantic high, with the sea state as calm as the Atlantic gets. As the 'nav' remembered it, several of the bombs exploded on hitting the sea. His crew carried out several of these trips over the period, the bombs being brought in from an unknown location a couple at a time. Airborne times were between 5 hours 20 minutes and 6 hours for the sorties.

While ED932, of course, had been Wg Cdr Guy Gibson's aircraft on the famous raid, ED906 was also very notable. This was the B.III (Special) flown by Flt Lt D.J.H. Maltby on Operation Chastise – then AJ-J and, of course, the aircraft which released the 'Upkeep' that actually breached the Möhne Dam.

On 17 May 1974 – the 31st anniversary of the Dam Busters raid – Lord Lilford unveiled a plaque and officially handed over NX611 to RAF Scampton's Station Commander Gp Capt J.B. Fitzpatrick. To round off the ceremony, PA474 carried out a flypast over the newly placed gate guard. Displayed in front of the Lancaster were examples of the special Barnes Wallis-designed weaponry carried by the type – a 12,000lb Tallboy, a 22,000lb Grand Slam and later on a trials version of the 'bouncing bomb'.

In 1983 some doubt again crept in with regard to the future of NX611. The end of the ten-year

Harold (left) and Fred Panton MBE.

loan period agreed by Lord Lilford was fast approaching, and various parties were interested in buying the Lanc. Among them were Fred and Harold Panton, who had been interested at the time of the Blackpool auction and had also been involved in the negotiations which eventually took NX611 to Scampton. The Lincolnshire farming brothers purchased the Lancaster from Lord Lilford on 1 September 1983. Its future secure, the Lanc remained on gate-guard duties at Scampton until May 1988, having spent almost fourteen years there.

One member of the team involved in moving NX611 away from Scampton was Mark Fletcher, who after many years of volunteering at East Kirkby is now a full-time employee there. Mark was posted straight from training as an aircraft mechanic (airframes) to the Aircraft Salvage and Transportation Flight at RAF Abingdon in December 1987.

The task of dismantling the Lancaster from its position as gate guard at RAF Scampton began around the end of March or beginning of April 1988. The Lancaster had to be moved onto the newly constructed car-parking area opposite the guardroom in order for there to be a firm hardstanding for all the heavy ground equipment, such as trestles, jacks and safety raisers.

The first major components to be removed were the outboard engines and all four propeller assemblies. The next major components to be removed were the fins and rudders, and then, once the two inboard engines had been removed, the remaining tailplane was disconnected. This was important because of the distribution of weight prior to raising the aircraft on jacks.

NX611 was then raised on jacks and trestles forward of the bomb bay and under the tail, with the outer wings also supported. Then the main wheels and bomb doors were removed and the process of disconnecting the wings outboard of the inner engines began. During this time the engines had been placed in transportation cradles inside the main gate perimeter wire, which runs parallel to the A15 road.

It was at this time that an enterprising scrap-metal dealer passed by and apparently assumed that the team was scrapping the Lancaster – he offered £40 for each of the engines. When the work party had stopped laughing, they explained that they were not actually scrapping the Lanc, and that even if they had been his meagre offer of £40 each was a long way short of their actual value – though they didn't imagine at the time that the engines would ever run again.

At this stage trestles were placed underneath the wings just outboard of the inner engines in order that they could take the weight of the outer wings as they were disconnected. The port wing was removed first, while the starboard was steadied with a large trestle. The outer wings themselves are only attached with four bolts, but these took some persuasion to come out. By then the Lanc looked very strange minus its outer wings, engines and tailplane.

NX611 while on gate-guard duties at RAF Scampton, photographed on 20 January 1984. Note the Tallboy, Grand Slam and Upkeep bombs on display in front of the Lanc.
(Duncan Cubitt)

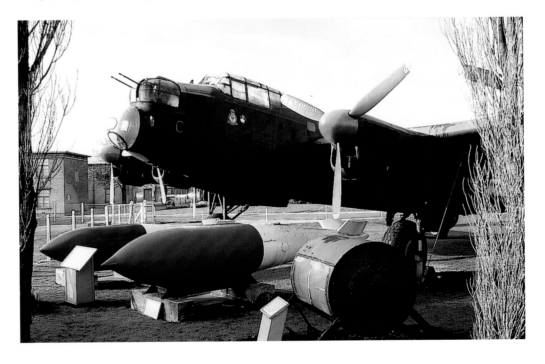

An unusual view of NX611 from directly behind, with a skull and crossbones emblem visible on the bottom of the rear turret.
(Duncan Cubitt)

The next stage involved separating the 69ft-long fuselage into three smaller chunks. This meant disconnecting the forward fuselage in front of the main spar, and the rear fuselage aft of the rear wing spar. At this point it became apparent that nearly fourteen years standing guard over RAF Scampton in all weathers had not been kind to the old Lanc. For the road move to East Kirkby, a distance of roughly thirty miles, it was decided that the rear fuselage needn't be broken down further (there is a further transportation joint roughly midway along the rear fuselage).

The wings were loaded onto trailers and commenced the journey to their new home. Most of the other major components had already been taken across to East Kirkby in the preceding weeks. Once the final sections of fuselage had been removed, the site was cleared and the Lancaster had left RAF Scampton.

It was ironic that the bomber arrived at East Kirkby from Scampton: 57 Sqn had been based at Scampton prior to moving to East Kirkby in 1943. And indeed it was from a nucleus of 57 Sqn airmen that the famous 617 Sqn had been formed earlier that same year.

When everything was in place, the task of putting the Lancaster back together began. Firstly, the major components such as wings and fuselage sections were unloaded and placed on trestles in roughly the correct position so that the aircraft looked rather like a large model kit. All the ground equipment then had to be moved into position, and with the assistance of two huge cranes the actual joining together of the sections began, starting with the main spar (centre section) and rear fuselage; then the forward fuselage, outer wings and tailplane.

NX611 has its Merlins opened up during one of East Kirkby's regular Lancaster running days, with the inboards caught running at 2,000rpm.

119

Some of the East Kirkby ground crew team. From left to right: Bill Parsons, Ian Hickling, Dave Stubley, Mark Fletcher, Roy Jarman and Pat Ellis.

Next the undercarriage was refitted. The main undercarriage wheels had been removed but the legs themselves had been folded into their undercarriage bays and fastened up. Now the Lanc was back on its feet again and was beginning to assume that familiar shape once more. Finally, the engines, rudders, propeller assemblies and last of all the engine cowlings were refitted – the Lancaster was complete and looked very much at home in its new purpose-built hangar.

The whole operation took the team from Abingdon approximately four months to complete. When first told that they would be moving the Lancaster from RAF Scampton to a

Chief Engineer Ian Hickling looks out over Nos 3 and 4 engines just before NX611 begins a taxi demonstration. On its starboard forward fuselage the Lanc wears the Bomber Command badge and the name and coat of arms of Sheffield. Although everybody generally refers to NX611 as *Just Jane*, the Lanc was additionally named *City of Sheffield* on 19 August 1995 in commemoration of all those who were employed in Sheffield's steelworks during the war, of the miners in the surrounding area who provided fuel for the war effort, and also as a tribute to all the citizens of Sheffield who endured the bombing of the city. Fred and Harold Panton were living near Sheffield when war broke out.

Looking out at rural Lincolnshire over NX611's Nos 3 and 4 engines as the Lancaster turns at the museum's far hardstanding.

farm belonging to two poultry farmers, some of the team were a little puzzled . . .

Following the arrival and reassembly of NX611 at East Kirkby, it received some cosmetic attention and was given the codes of the former bomber station's two resident Lancaster squadrons, Nos 57 and 630. This saw the bomber applied with a 57 Sqn DX-C code to starboard and a 630 Sqn LE-C code to port.

Having become co-owners of NX611 and responsible for establishing the Lincolnshire Aviation Heritage Centre, Fred and Harold's long-held wish to pay tribute to Christopher and all his fellow Bomber Command airmen was now

a reality. But during early 1993 they became confirmed in their opinion that it shouldn't remain just a static exhibit.

Former RAF engineers Ian Hickling and Roy Jarman were recruited, and in January 1994 they began the task of, one by one, coaxing the four Rolls-Royce Merlins back to life. Within just three months the No. 3 engine (starboard inner) was fit to run. A first tentative start-up was carried out on 20 April, the first time one of the aircraft's engines had been run since the Blackpool auction in 1972. It was followed by a

longer run, which was open to the public, the next evening.

It took just another three months before the No. 2 engine (port inner) was ready to run. This was fired up on 28 July, and the opportunity was also taken to start No. 3 and see the two inboard engines running together.

The following autumn and winter were spent overhauling various other systems, including the brakes – thoughts had now turned to NX611 actually being able to taxi under its own power. By the spring of 1995 the bomber was ready to

Having just signalled the ground crew for 'chocks away' before a taxi run in July 2003, 'Jacko' awaits clearance to move off. NX611's *Just Jane* name and nose art on the port side was inspired by the 1940s comic-strip character from the *Daily Mirror*.

NX611 stands quiet after one of its wonderfully atmospheric night-time taxi runs during November 1999. Watching one of these manoeuvres offers visitors a totally captivating experience, and one they will talk about for some time to come.

attempt this milestone. With both inboards running, on 4 March BBMF Lancaster pilot Flt Lt Mike Chatterton carefully eased the throttles forward and NX611 moved under its own power for the first time since February 1971.

Next to be operational was the No. 1 engine (port outer), which was started for the first time on 6 April 1995. To celebrate NX611's 50th birthday, later the same month, on 22 April, the bomber carried out its first public taxi run in front a large and appreciative crowd. The No. 4 engine (starboard outer) burst into life just under three months later, and on 13 August the Lancaster's first four-engined taxi run was

carried out, complete with a series of flypasts by PA474.

Generally speaking, a taxi run by *Just Jane* will go something like this. With the Lancaster facing away from the museum, the engines will be fired up: No. 3 first, then No. 4, followed by No. 2 and finally No. 1. After the engines have been warmed up, the flaps will be raised and the bomb doors closed. The external power will be disconnected and there will then be a wait until the coolant temperature reaches 40°C.

Once all is OK, the Lanc will move off and stop briefly within around five feet to check the brakes. The bomber will then trundle away under the supervision of its ground crew, who will marshal it to the bottom of the site where there is an area of hardstanding. It will then turn through 180° to face the crowd.

All four engines are brought up to 1,200rpm and the oil pressures are checked. With all reading OK, the inboard engines will be brought up to 2,000rpm by its engineer Ian Hickling for between a minute and a minute and a half. The pilot will then power up the outboards to 2,000rpm for a similar length of time as Ian powers down the inboards. The outboards are dropped back down and all the engines are left to sit at 1,200rpm for 15 to 20 seconds. The outboards are brought to idle at 600rpm and the inboards lowered to 1,000rpm. The bomber then taxies back towards its audience in the main square of the museum.

Once positioned roughly level with the control tower, all the engines are again brought up to 1,200rpm. Then the inboards are powered up to 2,000rpm again for one to one and a half minutes. Once more the outboards are powered up to 2,000rpm as the inboards are throttled back to 1,200rpm. They are again left like this for one to one and a half minutes, before being dropped back to 1,200rpm. The outboards are dropped to 600rpm and the inboards to 1,000rpm, ready for

the final taxi back into the parking position. Ian lowers the flaps to 50°, and once in place and fully stopped all four Merlins are brought up to 1,200rpm, which at close quarters gives the crowd a real taste of their power as the sound reverberates around the museum buildings. The bomb doors are opened and all the engines are shut down. It's just fantastic!

While such a sight is impressive enough, I was also privileged to be able to witness a tail-up fast taxi 'take-off' run by NX611 on 14 February 2002. NX611 was run down the remainder of East Kirkby's former runway at power enough to lift the tail wheel clear of the ground. The amazing sight of the Lincolnshire Aviation Heritage Centre's Lanc performing these runs was courtesy of a BBC filming contract which would include the bomber in a new drama to be screened in the autumn of that year.

NX611 was towed across to the runway from the museum with the aid of 250ft of corrugated aluminium matting laid over field areas. What is left of the runway has fortunately been maintained in good order over the years.

This day was used for a series of test runs prior to filming in order to establish the power settings needed to get the rear wheel off the ground and where to shut off in order to stop in good time. The runway was measured and found to give a total length of just under 4,500ft. Green flags were placed every 500ft of its length for safety reasons to give the crew, pilot Mike Chatterton and engineer Ian Hickling (both of whom have served with BBMF), accurate markers as to where power would need to be shut down.

On initial runs the Lancaster was just taxied up and down the length in order to test that all systems were working satisfactorily, especially the brakes. Once it was established that all was well, NX611 set off down the runway into wind at a speed never before possible for the taxiable Lanc while owned by under Fred and Harold Panton.

With the propeller of No. 2 engine spinning furiously behind him, former OC BBMF Sqn Ldr Ken Jackson MBE, AFC, is seen in the pilot's seat during an engine run at the far end of the Lancaster's taxi area within the museum site.

The rear wheel lifted clear of the ground after only about 80ft of travel. After running with the tail in the air for about 18 seconds, the power was cut and the Lancaster brought to a safe stop with plenty of room to spare. NX611 was then taxied back up the runway for a second trip. This, too, went very smoothly, and the sight of a Lancaster looking as though it was about to take off from this former 57 and 630 Sqn airfield, with little on hand to give away the true date, transcended ideas of time.

For the first two runs the outboard engines were set at 2,200rpm and zero boost, with the inboard engines set at 2,500rpm and +4 boost. For one final trip later in the afternoon it was decided to increase power slightly and give the inboard engines +5 boost.

Some 'present day' footage was filmed at the museum on 18 February, and the Second World War 'take-off run' filming began on the 21st. For this work, NX611 was given some slight cosmetic changes. Most noticeable was that it lost its *Just*

After the first series of engine power-ups, NX611 taxies back in towards the main museum site, much to the delight of the visitors. The superbly restored control tower is visible above the spinners, and the building to the right of the picture is the memorial chapel, inside which can be found the rolls of honour listing all those who gave their lives while operating out of East Kirkby during the Second World War.

In the hands of pilot Mike Chatterton, NX611 roars down the runway at East Kirkby wearing CM-V codes for film work. Also note that NX611 is minus its popular *Just Jane* name and nose art, which was temporarily painted over to give the bomber anonymity during the filming.
(Duncan Cubitt)

Jane nose art, and instead featured only its bomb tally and victory markings. Also, the Lancaster lost its usual DX-C and LE-C codes, and instead gained CM-V markings on both sides. The CM-code was used to provide a fictitious squadron identity, though in reality it was allocated to 107 (Transport) Operational Training Unit, Leicester East, in March 1944. All these changes were only temporary, though, and NX611 soon

reverted to its *Just Jane* guise following the filming work.

The drama was entitled *Night Flight*, and starred Christopher Plummer and Edward Woodward as Second World War veterans whose memories still haunted them. It told the moving story of Harry Peters (played by Christopher Plummer), an RAF veteran who at the age of twenty piloted a Lancaster. At a present-day

Remembrance Day commemoration, Harry, by then a pensioner, had his world turned upside down when a former comrade, Vic Green (Edward Woodward), came back into his life. Vic introduced Harry to the son of their rear gunner, who had been killed in the war. Desperate to keep a lid on the past and its secrets, Harry tried to keep his distance; but memories kept flooding back and long-repressed emotions threatened to destroy him before old ghosts could finally be laid to rest.

BBC Controller of Drama Commissioning, Jane Tranter, commented at the time: 'We are proud to be making this powerful drama which captures the unique and terrifying experience of flying a Lancaster bomber, and explores the impact on those still living with these memories today.'

Sqn Ldr 'Jacko' Jackson (left) and Ian Hickling working in unison to demonstrate the sight and sound of four Merlins being throttled up. The video camera at top right was present to record this taxi run from inside the cockpit for the latest in a series of documentary programmes on the Lancaster, its owners and the museum.

Ian Hickling monitors NX611's flight engineer's panel to check that all temperatures are within limits before the bomber is taxied.

What the filming brought to Lincolnshire was the sight of a Lancaster on East Kirkby's runway for the first time since around 1946, plus the first time NX611's tail wheel had been lifted into the air under its own power since the 1971 film work at Blackpool. And with 14 February traditionally set aside as a date for passion, it was apt that many pulses were set racing on that gloriously sunny day as a classic British bomber set off down a historic Lincolnshire airfield as if to take off on another perilous op.

As well as Mike Chatterton, NX611's pilots also include Sqn Ldr Ken 'Jacko' Jackson MBE AFC and Sqn Ldr Rick Groombridge. All three are former BBMF Lancaster pilots, and two of them have even served as Officer Commanding!

In the year following the filming of *Night Flight*, on 6 September 2003, Jacko celebrated his 80th birthday in a truly unique manner – by becoming the only 80-year-old pilot ever to taxi an Avro Lancaster! He has been taxiing NX611 since 1994.

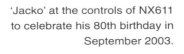

'Jacko' at the controls of NX611 to celebrate his 80th birthday in September 2003.

Following his 80th birthday taxi run, 'Jacko' was presented with a rather appropriately decorated birthday cake!

After the taxi run, East Kirkby's NAAFI was used for a party in honour of Jacko, who was presented with a framed picture and a specially made birthday cake – decorated with an edible picture of *Just Jane* printed on the top!

When asked what this significant achievement and taxiing *Just Jane* still means to him, Sqn Ldr Jackson replied: 'It is a wonderful experience and a privileged way to end my aviation career.'

Ian Hickling and Roy Jarman, who worked so hard to make all this a reality, can still be found carefully looking after NX611 at East Kirkby. Ian always rides with the Lanc as flight engineer. Today they are ably assisted by a ground crew team including Kev Baker, Andy Coupland, Pat Ellis, Mark Fletcher, Bill Parsons and Dave Stubley.

Of course, it is also very important to mention that not only can visitors get close to NX611 as they watch it taxi around during one of the Lancaster's running days at East Kirkby, but they can actually pay to go for a ride! Spaces are limited and are often booked up well in advance, so if you would like this experience of a lifetime call the relevant number included in the appendix listing Lancaster survivors.

Just Jane's taxi runs are very popular, and large crowds flock to East Kirkby to see them. As autumn approaches, it gets towards the time for my personal favourite attraction at East Kirkby to begin – the night-time taxi demonstrations. These offer visitors the opportunity to see a Lancaster with all four engines running in its natural environment, with the added bonus of being able to see flames flashing out of the exhaust stubs.

Visits to the site are made all the more fascinating by the rest of the museum's collection and other attractions. These include airworthy Supermarine Spitfire Tr.IX MJ627 (which regularly flies from East Kirkby in the hands of former OC BBMF Sqn Ldr Paul Day OBE AFC),

NX611 carrying out night-time engine runs in November 2004. Using a tripod for the camera, the movement of the propellers is exaggerated in this photograph due to an exposure time of six seconds.

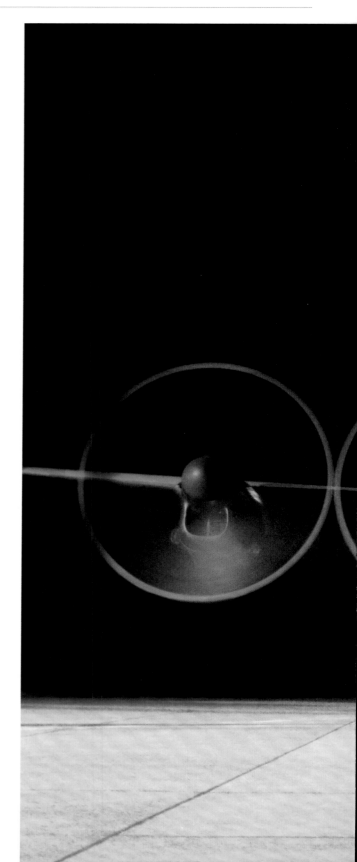

Below: East Kirkby's pleasant museum site offers visitors splendid views of the taxiable Lancaster.

Opposite: Mike Chatterton (visible to the right of the picture in the pilot's seat) and Ian Hickling while carrying out a taxi run in *Just Jane*. (Duncan Cubitt)

the restoration project of HP Hampden I AE436, the superbly restored control tower, the memorial chapel and roll of honour plus a great NAAFI!

The family-run museum is the result of years of determination and commitment. Fred and Harold's tremendous work to honour their elder brother and the many other Bomber Command airmen lost during the Second World War was rightly recognised when Fred was named in the 2003 New Year's Honours List for Services to Aviation Heritage, becoming Fred Panton MBE.

As the period music plays around the site, and as you hear the communications inside the control tower and then revel at the sight and sound of four Merlins erupting into life, you could be forgiven for thinking you've stepped back in time . . .

The one question which is continually being asked of Fred and Harold concerns if and when the Lanc is going to fly. So I cannot conclude this chapter on *Just Jane* without mention of it, and there's no better way than with this letter which the brothers kindly wrote for me after an influx of enquiries to the magazine following the news story and photographs of the Lancaster with its tail wheel lifted clear of the ground:

Like many of you, we congratulate Duncan Cubitt for the excellent photographs of Avro Lancaster NX611 *Just Jane* doing her stuff by lifting her tail clear of the runway after more than thirty years. She was in the capable hands of pilot Flt Lt Mike Chatterton, engineer Ian Hickling, and not forgetting Roy Jarman. A moving sight indeed, the Merlin engines responding to the challenge with a spirit-stirring roar.

We are frequently being asked, 'When is she going to fly?' A fair question, our honest answer is we don't know. We have no immediate plans to go airworthy, but it is, we believe, possible.

Since NX611 came to East Kirkby in 1988, much work has been done to the aircraft's engines, controls, hydraulics, brakes and much more. All has been carried out on a 'one step at a time' policy over the years, and now it seems a big step forward is presenting itself to us. There is no lack of enthusiasm or commitment, though at the same time realistic 'for and against' thoughts come to mind.

Lancaster NX611 has been nurtured back to life. She has felt the air under and over her wings again – she just might one day! And what a sight that would be. We'll keep you posted. Thank you all for your interest, best wishes and support.

Fred and Harold Panton

At the entrance to the Lincolnshire Aviation Heritage Centre is a thoughtful memorial to all those who gave their lives while serving with 57 and 630 Sqns during the Second World War.

CHAPTER 5

W4783 – Australian War Memorial

Having been fascinated by the Avro Lancaster for as long as I can remember, I particularly enjoy seeing how the various survivors are presented for display. In the UK that means PA474, the Battle of Britain Memorial Flight's star turn; NX611, which regularly carries out taxi runs at the Lincolnshire Aviation Heritage Centre; R5868 at the RAF Museum London; and KB889 at the Imperial War Museum Duxford in Cambridgeshire. These wonderful aircraft offer a simply superb range of display attributes – everything from an airworthy example, through a taxiable bomber often seen moving under its own power at night, to superbly presented static museum showpieces.

460 SQUADRON
ROYAL AUSTRALIAN AIR FORCE

To COMMEMORATE RECORD LANCASTER AIRCRAFT

"G" for GEORGE

COMPLETED SEVENTY-NINE OPERATIONS
OVER ENEMY OCCUPIED COUNTRIES - 5TH Jan., 1944.

As well as the mission marks on W4783's operations tally, the Lancaster's exploits were recorded for posterity in a series of small plaques produced by one of the men who maintained it, instrument-maker LAC Len Priestley. This example, from operation seventy-nine, was kindly loaned to me by Erica Straw, whose grandfather, Flt Sgt John Bailey, served with 460 Sqn as a bomb aimer from January 1944. After John died, the plaque was given to Erica by her grandmother, Mrs Sylvia Bailey. Family interest is furthered by the fact that Erica is married to BBMF Lancaster pilot Flt Lt Ed Straw, who regularly flies the RAF's PA474 as a tribute to Bomber Command aircrew.
(Courtesy Erica Straw)

A number of 'Back Them Up!' posters are displayed in front of W4783. Produced in their thousands, these were pasted up in prominent places all over Britain – street hoardings, railway stations, bus stops and London Underground stations. They were designed to promote the Air Force, Army and Navy and to enlist public support by encouraging them to buy war bonds, volunteer for services and help increase wartime production. Air Force 'Back Them Up!' posters depicted the principal types of bomber aircraft carrying out raids over Germany.
(Duncan Cubitt)

The R.A.F.'s intensive bombing of Germany's war industries continues.

BACK THEM UP!

W4783's 'bomb log' has been impressively reproduced as part of the historically accurate repaint.
(Duncan Cubitt)

But on the other side of the globe, during December 2003, something very different was unleashed on the public. After a meticulous five-year restoration, Lancaster I W4783 AR-G *G-for-George* was put back on display to form the centrepiece of an extraordinary light-and-sound show at the Australian War Memorial in Canberra, Australian Capital Territory. Having studied Lancaster survivors with such a passion, I really just had to see this for myself.

The display's title, 'Striking by Night', gave me some indication of what was in store, and visitors were given their first chance to experience the full effect on 6 December 2003. Using extremely imaginative and convincing lighting and sound effects, and backed up by archive and computer-generated film, the display cleverly re-creates a wartime bomber operation to Berlin during 1943.

G-for-George is a memorial to all the Australian airmen who lost their lives over Europe during the Second World War. The aircraft served with 460 Sqn RAAF, a unit that alone carried out some 6,264 operational sorties while based at various stations, including Breighton, Yorkshire

This view from the top gallery at the AWM shows *G-for-George* in its atmospheric 'Striking by Night' environment.
(Duncan Cubitt)

and later Binbrook, Lincolnshire – both of which were home to W4783.

This Lancaster was built by Metropolitan-Vickers Ltd at Mosley Road, Manchester, in mid-1942. It was taken on charge by the RAF on 22 October 1942, and was one of the first Lancasters delivered to 460 Sqn, which was, at that time, based at Breighton.

The squadron was manned mostly by Australians, and its outstanding contribution to the war effort has earned it a very special place in the country's aviation heritage. The unit flew more missions, dropped more bombs, received more decorations and suffered more casualties than any other Australian squadron – indeed, any in Bomber Command.

Assigned the code UV-G, *G-for-George* flew its first mission on the night of 6 December 1942 over Mannheim, Germany. Around May 1943 the squadron code changed, and W4783 became AR-G. In total this Lanc completed ninety bombing operations with various crews, the last

of which took place on 10 April 1944 – its destination was Cologne.

As was common wartime practice, each of the ops were recorded on the aircraft's port forward fuselage. But in addition to the bomb silhouettes, there are some other interesting features on *G-for-George*.

The first fifteen silhouettes are each accompanied by a stick figure of The Saint, based on the Simon Templar character of the contemporary novels that were later popularised by the British TV series. These represent ops piloted by Flt Sgt James Alec 'The Saint' Saint-Smith (however, there is some confusion here, as the second and third ops were recorded as being flown by Flt Sgt A.F. McKinnon). Other bomb markings feature a red diagonal stripe, representing those flown by Flt Sgt Jack Murray and crew.

After the thirty-third op there is a Soviet flag, and there are several explanations for the addition of this. The one thought the most likely, though, is that it denotes the raid on Stettin which took place 20 April 1943, which was flown to help the Russians. However, the mystery doesn't end quite so simply. The squadron's operations books record the Stettin raid as the aircraft's thirty-second op, not the thirty-third as marked on the bomb tally. This may lead to belief in a different explanation of the flag's presence, which is that around the time of its addition there was a move to redeclare and popularise the Allies, especially the USSR.

There is still further confusion, too, as the flag does in fact differ slightly from the flag of the Soviet Union; the reason being that it was thought at the time that there could be repercussions if a communist flag was painted on a British aircraft. So a definitive explanation about why this flag was added to W4783's bomb log may never come to light.

There are also blue 'victory' symbols above the missions flown by Fg Off James R. Henderson.

The bomber's crew were inspired by Sir Winston Churchill's famous 'V for Victory' sign, embodied in the blue 'V' markings, which gave them a comforting feeling of hope and duty.

A pair of cherries appear above the twenty-one bomb symbols of Plt Off Harry Carter's crew. This motif depicted the pilot's nickname from his training days at Wagga, New South Wales: he was called 'Cherry' because he was then so innocent. However, Harry's crew went on to fly more ops in *G-for-George* than any other – by

At Binbrook village in Lincolnshire there is a memorial to 460 Sqn. This picture of it was deliberately taken after dark to fit in with the 'Striking by Night' theme.

which time he was over blushing when spoken to by a girl!

Perhaps the most intriguing additions, though, are the three medal ribbons, one painted after every thirty operations. These were unofficial 'honorary' decorations awarded to *G-for-George* by the aircraft's ground crew. The first is the Distinguished Flying Medal, the second the Conspicuous Gallantry Medal and the third the Distinguished Service Order.

In November 1943, a letter was sent from RAAF Headquarters to 460 Sqn, by then based at Binbrook, asking if there was a suitable Lancaster that could be displayed in the AWM to commemorate the sacrifices of Australian airmen. *G-for-George* fitted the bill perfectly: it was thought to be the oldest Lanc still in operational service, had already been suggested for preservation, had achieved a high number of operations

(seventy at that time), and had mainly been flown by Australian crews.

The squadron's CO at the time, Sqn Ldr F.A. Arthur DFC, put forward W4783 as a candidate and suggested it should be flown around Australia for publicity purposes. It was proposed that a crew which had completed two operational tours, should sail with the Lanc to Australia so that they would be in place to fly it around the country once it had been made ready. The idea was accepted in principle, and *G-for-George* was earmarked for preservation still with some months of operational service ahead of it.

George survived a further twenty ops and, following retirement, its official transfer was made on 20 May 1944. Australia's Prime Minister, The Rt Hon. John Curtin, travelled to Binbrook to accept *G-for-George* on behalf of the Australian people.

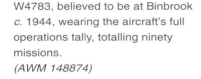

W4783, believed to be at Binbrook *c.* 1944, wearing the aircraft's full operations tally, totalling ninety missions.
(AWM 148874)

By then it had also been decided that W4783 should be flown to Australia, as there was some great public-relations material to be gained from a war veteran undertaking such a marathon trip. Thus on 29 May *G-for-George* flew from Binbrook to Waddington, Lincolnshire, where Avro carried out a major overhaul which included fitting long-range fuel tanks into the bomb bay.

Initially, it was decided that the Lanc should be flown to Australia by Sqn Ldr Eric Jarman DFC and his crew. However, they were shot down and posted missing, presumed dead, on 28 April 1944. It was later discovered there was just one survivor from the crew.

Flt Lt Edward Arthur Hudson DFC* and his crew were then chosen to make the trip. Between them, these men had as much experience and were as highly decorated as any other Australian crew serving in England. *George* left Binbrook for the last time on 6 October 1944, and set off for Prestwick, Scotland, from where it would begin the flight to Australia on 11 October. The Lanc touched down on Australian soil at Amberley airfield near Brisbane on 8 November – ten days late and having spent around seventy-eight hours in the air.

Some months later *G-for-George* participated in the Third Victory Loan Tour, which began on 13 March 1945 and lasted until the end of April.

W4783 is pictured on arrival at Temora on 28 March 1945, during the Third Victory Loan Tour. *(Courtesy Temora Aviation Museum)*

Behind W4783 can be seen one of the two large screens that show film footage during the feature presentation.
(Duncan Cubitt)

144

The aim was to boost the war effort by encouraging members of the public to buy war bonds. At numerous venues, anyone who invested £100 in bonds was rewarded with a local flight, usually lasting around thirty minutes, with around thirty passengers being accommodated on each trip. Inspections of the interior were granted to those spending £10 or more on bonds. For this reason the Lanc was also officially designated a transport aircraft. The tour began at Melbourne and took in various locations including Adelaide, Deniliquin, Sydney and Brisbane.

Interestingly, one of the venues on this tour was Temora, now home to the Temora Aviation Museum and its superb collection of airworthy warbirds. The Lanc landed there on 28 March and undertook a passenger flight that afternoon. And in December 2003 G-for-George's return to display was paid a tribute by two aircraft from the museum as they carried out a flypast to celebrate the opening of 'Striking by Night'.

On completion of the tour the Lanc had raised £319,870 for the war effort. But, additionally, G-for-George had helped to whip up considerable patriotic fervour.

W4783 made its last flight on 24 September 1945, when it flew to the RAAF base at Canberra, close to the AWM. No long-term hangar space was available at the time, so the AWM was asked to take charge of the aircraft as soon as possible – but there was no room at the Memorial either. As a result, G-for-George spent almost ten years parked outside in a less than secure part of the airfield, during which time it suffered from exposure to the elements and was robbed of many interior fittings.

Its rapidly declining state attracted some unfavourable press attention, so in the mid-1950s hangar space was finally found. Once inside, some repairs were carried out and a new lick of paint was applied. However, demand for hangar space was still high at the RAAF base, so by June 1955 G-for-George had been dismantled, moved into the AWM, and reassembled for display in its Aeroplane Hall.

During 1999, a major redevelopment of the memorial's aircraft displays saw the Lancaster removed from what was then called the Bradbury Aircraft Hall. G-for-George needed some urgent attention: as well as its deteriorating paintwork, it was suffering from corrosion, metal fatigue and a cracked main undercarriage support. It was once again disassembled, and moved to the AWM's workshop for a complete conservation project that would include repairs to the airframe and refitting the long-since-missing components. All this would be rounded off with a historically accurate repaint.

The restoration took thirty staff and volunteers five years to complete. During this time it was extensively disassembled and thoroughly cleaned and treated. To ensure the new scheme would be totally accurate, the paint was carefully rubbed back to reveal the original wartime colours and designs. This process revealed small red swastikas on the front of each spinner, and for accuracy these have once again been applied to the Lanc.

Other fascinating finds included wartime propaganda leaflets, a 1942 halfpenny, and even some original signatures from the 'war bond' tour inscribed on the interior. Great pains were taken to save as many of the latter as possible during the aircraft's conservation.

The finished result is a superbly turned-out Lancaster that achieves the AWM's goal, 'to commemorate the exceptional service (and appalling casualty rates) of Australians in Bomber Command'. And now, at the centre of the new 'Striking by Night' display in the AWM's Anzac Hall, visitors can see G-for-George undertake a virtual mission to Berlin, based on op seventy-three, which took place on 16 December 1943.

'Striking by Night' opened to the public on the very appropriate date of 6 December 2003 –

145

W4783 has a representative display of various bomb types underneath it, including a replica Cookie bomb, placed as though about to be winched into the bomb bay.
(Duncan Cubitt)

sixty-one years to the day since *G-for-George* had embarked on its first mission. Upwards of 2,000 people, including Bomber Command veterans and representatives of the government and military, made the trip to Canberra to mark *George*'s return to public display.

Three Messerschmitts are also on display near the Lanc: a Bf 109, an Me 163 and an Me 262. Bf 109G-2 163824 is pole-mounted off to *George*'s port wingtip, and notably still wears its original wartime paintwork. It took eight months

of concentrated effort to stabilise and preserve this historic finish, clean the aircraft and replace the canopy's broken Perspex. A replacement tail wheel had to be purchased from Belgium, and the armament is missing, but otherwise the aircraft is complete.

While the Me 163 and '262 are located in a small gallery behind the Lanc, the Bf 109, which until then had never before been on public display, plays a key role in 'Striking by Night', as will become clear.

The experience has been designed so that visitors can learn about the Allies' bombing strategy and its effects, something that is brought closer to home by individual stories of courage and sacrifice. A variety of perspectives are considered, from young crews flying nightly over the most heavily defended targets in Europe and twenty-year-old pilots bringing home badly damaged bombers, to ground personnel including WAAFs, the families waiting at home, and those who were under the falling bombs.

At the time of my visit the 'Striking by Night' presentation was being run on the hour, every hour. As the re-creation begins, the area around *G-for-George* darkens and narration sets the scene: 'On transfer to a station in England, I discovered there were dark-blue uniforms everywhere. The ones I had noticed were mostly Australians. Life on the stations wasn't easy for the crews. We who waited for the aircraft to return knew a terrible sense of dread each time.' The words are taken from a letter sent to the AWM by Mrs Dorothy 'Paddy' Foran OAM, who served as a WAAF from 1942.

Rolls-Royce Merlins then roar into action as they fire up through the surround-sound system, while ingenious lighting effects simulate the propellers turning on *G-for-George*. Two screens are positioned behind the Lanc; in between the shows they display a rotating montage of wartime stills, but now they help to complete the atmosphere with period footage of Lancasters starting up. You begin to get a real sense of the tension that must have affected the crews as they prepared to set off on another raid.

After the Lancasters taxi out and take off, the sound fades to a simulation of the drone inside an aircraft to accompany the

images of Lancs in flight. You then see ops personnel plotting the formation's progress, and the narration tells us: 'In 1943 a massive aerial bombing campaign attempted to destroy Germany's industry and its will to fight. The losses of aircraft and crew were almost unsustainable. On the evening of 16 December 1943, Lancaster *G-for-George*, crewed mainly by Australians, was one of five hundred bombers headed for Berlin.'

As the Lancs reach altitude, the Australian captain checks with his crew members that they have their oxygen masks on: 'We're at ten thousand feet, check your oxygen.'

W4783 has mannequins placed in various crew positions, which add a further touch of realism during 'Striking by Night'. In the dark of the display area, the bomb aimer is illuminated to highlight his role to visitors looking up towards the bomber.
(Duncan Cubitt)

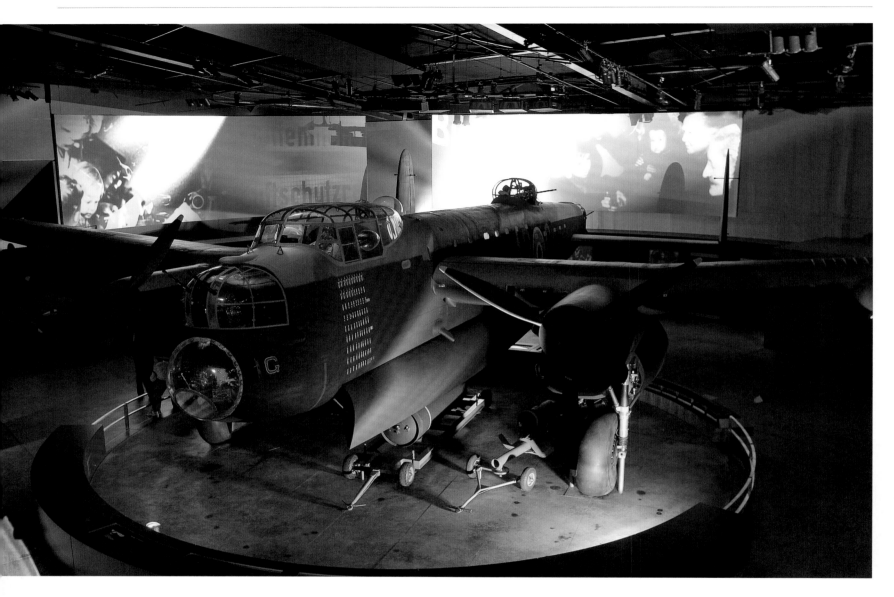

The first of several views from the captivating 'Striking by Night' display, showing the range of lighting and visual effects that help to re-create the tension of a Lancaster bombing op in 1943. *(Duncan Cubitt)*

With the lights then focusing on each respective position in turn to direct the attention of the audience, each member of the crew answers his skipper.

'Bomb aimer here, oxygen OK.'
'Engineer, oxygen OK.'
'Navigator's fine.'
'Wireless op OK.'
'Mid-upper OK, skipper.'
'Rear gunner OK.'

The radio chatter continues with the voice of the navigator: 'We are at our rendezvous position. Keep on this course and we will reach the Dutch coast near Ijmuiden.'

'Understood, navigator,' replies the pilot.

'Navigator to bomb aimer, tell me when we pass the coast and if you see any lights.'

The bomb aimer replies: 'Navigator, we are passing over the coast now but no lights – too much cloud cover.'

'Navigator to skipper. At the turn, estimated time to Berlin on this course, two hours.'

As *George* nears an area where there is a risk that night-fighters may intercept, the navigator again gives out instructions:

'Approaching area of heavy night-fighter cover. Bomb aimer, start unloading your bundles of Window.'

As the screens show an aircraft releasing 'Window' (small metal strips to confuse the radar), the bomb aimer calls out: 'I am throwing out Window now.'

Then the navigator says: 'Can anyone see yellow flares?'

The mid-upper gunner calls out: 'Yellow flares ahead. There's also a whole line of fighter flares to port, and searchlights dead ahead.'

Then the bomb aimer screams out loud: 'Skipper, flak coming up to port, get weaving!'

The captain asks his crew to be observant: 'Keep an eye out for aircraft in the stream.'

In a moment the mid-upper gunner exclaims: 'Lanc going down to starboard. Bloody Hell!'

Coned by searchlights, the Lancaster becomes a prominent target in the night skies above Germany.
(Duncan Cubitt)

The screens show the crew at work during the tension of the bombing operation.
(Duncan Cubitt)

But the crew must keep their mind on the task in hand, as the navigator states: 'Estimated position over target fifteen minutes at 2005hr, right on time.'

At the same time that the audience hears all this, an impression of blinding searchlights, flares and anti-aircraft fire has been beamed around the dark auditorium.

As the Lanc approaches the target, air-raid sirens bellow out as the audience is taken to ground level. Spotlights illuminate the 88mm anti-aircraft gun that forms part of the display. The screens show civilians running through the streets of Berlin for the safety of the shelters, and the order goes out to scramble the night-fighters.

A Pathfinder crew make a call on the radio after dropping the target indicators: 'Pathfinder Force to all aircraft. Some reds are scattered to the south. All aircraft are to bomb on the greens.'

George's pilot calls the bomb aimer: 'Approaching target. Take it, bomb aimer.'

The bomb aimer replies: 'Come left on the greens, skipper. Left, left, steady. Bomb doors open. Right, steady, hold it. Bombs gone!'

The screens then show a mass of blast effects, and the lighting turns a startling red as the audience considers the carnage below. Searchlights cone around the auditorium walls as the Lanc heads for its plot. 'Turning point coming up in one minute.'

G-for-George then succumbs to an attack from the Bf 109, and the rear gunner calls out: 'Fighter on starboard quarter. Corkscrew starboard, corkscrew starboard!' Again, this is cleverly re-created with flashing yellow lighting on the fighter's gun ports, convincingly accompanied by gunfire sound effects. *G-for-George*'s mid-upper guns also return fire.

The bomber stream is again caught in searchlights and fired at from the ground (left), before spotting the flares dropped by the Pathfinders (below).
(Duncan Cubitt)

Pilot: 'Are you OK, rear gunner?'

Gunner: 'Christ, that was close!'

The pilot asks: 'Any damage?'

Fortunately, the Lanc survives to press on for home.

There's a sense of relief for the captivated audience as the film shows Lancs returning home and the tension of the op begins to subside. But not all the aircraft in the stream are safe, as we realise when the bomb aimer calls out: 'Lanc burning to port.'

The radio chatter, film footage and sound effects all combine to replicate the return journey.

Navigator: 'England coming up, everybody keep a lookout for the coast.'

Bomb aimer: 'It's a nasty one tonight, can't see a bloody thing.'

G-for-George drops its payload as the auditorium turns a startling red. (*Duncan Cubitt*)

G-for-George makes a safe landing back at base, but then reality strikes home through the commentary: 'For the seventy-third time *George* had returned safely from an operation. But as the crews finished their early morning debriefings, it was obvious that the cost had been very high. Over fifty bombers were lost. This night became known as "Black Thursday".'

More emotive words from WAAF Dorothy Foran round off the presentation: 'My memories are of young men, "Aussie" men, laughing, dancing, singing and enjoying the moment, never to be heard of again; shot down or killed in action. They were young, handsome and full of life.'

Thoughts are provoked still further by the staggering statistics of Bomber Command losses – Australian and in total – which are displayed in silence at the end of the presentation. As the lights come back up you can't help but feel a sense of overwhelming gratitude to all those brave young airmen who made the ultimate sacrifice, and sadness for the loss felt by their families.

The whole experience is condensed into just under ten minutes, but in that short time your imagination is captivated by the conditions these aircraft operated under during the Second World War. Modern technology has been used to great effect, ensuring that 'Striking by Night' convincingly re-creates the tension and danger of a raid – it's an extraordinary experience. And just to confirm this, it's worth noting that soon after I wrote an article about this display I received a letter from a gentleman in Australia who had taken his father, who flew on Lancs during the war, to watch it. He just wanted to let me know that the realism of 'Striking by Night' was so accurate that it had actually brought back the feeling of going on an op to his father.

After I'd been back for a second look, I felt the most appropriate thing to do next was to pay my respects at the various war memorials along Anzac Parade, situated directly in front of the AWM. The Australian War Memorial is to be congratulated for presenting its Lancaster in a wholly different way that thoughtfully considers the human perspective of wartime operations. Its success can be measured by the fact that within a year of 'Striking by Night' being opened, visitor figures at the Memorial had risen by almost 30 per cent.

Visitors are left to consider the carnage below as the screens display fire teams attempting to contain the raging flames on the ground.
(Duncan Cubitt)

The main entrance of the Australian War Memorial. Just inside is the Pool of Reflection, at the far end of which is the Eternal Flame. The dome forms the roof of the Hall of Memory, which houses the Tomb of the Unknown Soldier.

This view from the top of Mount Ainslie shows the rear of the Australian War Memorial and its position directly at the top of Anzac Parade, which has various military memorials situated along the edges of the boulevard commemorating Australia's war efforts.
(Duncan Cubitt)

CHAPTER 6

R5868 – Royal Air Force Museum London

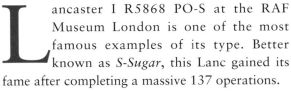

Lancaster I R5868 PO-S at the RAF Museum London is one of the most famous examples of its type. Better known as *S-Sugar*, this Lanc gained its fame after completing a massive 137 operations.

R5868 was built by Metropolitan-Vickers at its Mosley Road works in Manchester. On 29 June 1942 it was delivered to 83 Sqn at RAF Scampton, Lincolnshire, coded OL-Q and allocated to 'B' Flight. The squadron had begun converting from Avro Manchesters that April.

This Lancaster's first operational sortie came on the night of 8/9 July 1942, when it took part in a raid on Wilhelmshaven. With its 'Q' code, R5868 soon became known as *Queenie* and was quickly adorned with its first nose art – a nude female kneeling in front of a bomb, on the port side just aft of the front turret.

On 11 July *Queenie* participated in a dusk raid on submarine yards at Danzig. A total of forty-four Lancasters took part in this, the most distant raid yet made by Bomber Command against a German target. It involved a 1,500-mile round trip, and the sortie lasted a total of 10 hours 5 minutes.

Another notable sortie occurred on 18 August 1942, when R5868 participated in the first Pathfinder Force operation, against Flensburg, carrying flares only. However, hazy conditions meant that R5868 was one of four Lancs not to drop its flares. Most operations from then on saw this bomber flown as a Pathfinder.

The night of 16/17 January 1943 was the first of *Queenie*'s eight visits to Berlin, when again it carried only flares, most of which were brought back, as after twenty-five minutes over the target area the crew could not distinguish any pinpoints in the poor visibility. During another raid on Berlin, on 29/30 March, the aircraft suffered flak damage after being coned by searchlights for nine minutes.

R5868's fiftieth op occurred on the night of 29/30 May 1943 when it flew to Wuppertal and the bomber's sixty-eighth op on 15/16 August 1943 was its final sortie with 83 Sqn. By then R5868 had completed 450 flying hours, nearly 368 of which were operational.

In September 1943 the bomber was transferred to 467 Sqn at RAF Bottesford, Leicestershire. R5868 gained its now familiar code, PO-S, and

joined 'B' Flight as a replacement S-*Sugar*; JA981 had crashed in the North Sea on 15 September 1943. When R5868 joined 467 Sqn its kneeling-nude nose art was replaced by a red devil (Mephistopheles – to whom Faust sold his soul in German legend) thumbing its nose, dancing in flames with the motto 'Devils of the Air' beneath it. On 11 November 1943 the squadron moved to RAF Waddington in Lincolnshire, a base it would share with another Australian unit, 463 Sqn.

S-*Sugar* returned to Berlin again on 18/19 November 1943. This was the beginning of the 'Battle of Berlin', and R5868 was one of twenty 467 Sqn Lancasters in the raid. As *Sugar*'s bomb tally approached the 100 mark, the press began to take an interest, and higher authority decided that the devil would have to go. In its place was inscribed Herman Göring's vain boast: 'NO ENEMY PLANE WILL FLY OVER THE REICH TERRITORY'.

S-*Sugar* and its crew had a narrow escape during an operation in late November 1943, when it collided with a Lancaster from 61 Sqn at 20,000ft over Berlin. The two bombers came together as a result of them both taking evasive action after being coned by searchlights. The Squadron ORB recorded at the time: 'Flying Officer J.A. Colpus tried "Aussie Rules Football" with another Lancaster and tried to bump it out of the sky. The aircraft went into a severe dive to port, but by applying full rudder and aileron trim the aircraft straightened, though it still needed a lot of pressure on both the rudder pedals and the control column to maintain height. The aircraft was our old reliable S-*Sugar*, and it had completed nearly eighty trips. In this kite the pilot and navigator could go to sleep coming home, for it knows its way back from almost any target.' The collision occurred just after bombing the target, and the aircraft eventually landed at Tholthorpe, Yorkshire. Following repairs,

S-*Sugar* was back in action on 15/16 February 1944.

Around the time of its ninety-eighth operation, *Sugar* was adopted by girls of the sugar section of the Australian Rationing Commission, who wrote to the bomber's Australian crew. R5868 flew supposedly its 100th operation – actually its 102nd or 103rd, counting two early returns – on the night of 11/12 May 1944. The crew returned to Waddington to find the station waiting to toast the 'Centenarian', which had just survived ten determined attacks by a brace of Junkers Ju 88 night-fighters.

In February 1945 *Sugar* made a tour of USAAF bomber bases in East Anglia. It was flown by an Australian wing commander from 460 Sqn. This goodwill tour of 8th Air Force bases lasted six weeks. The tour began at Bovingdon, Hertfordshire, on the 10th, and bases visited included Great Ashfield, Woodbridge, Debden and Thorpe Abbots, home of the 100th Bomb Group.

Sugar's final operational sortie came on 23 April 1945, to Flensburg. No bombs were dropped on this due to thick 10/10 cloud. This was the bomber's 137th op, by the end of which it had flown around 800 operational hours and dropped 466 tons of bombs. The only RAF heavy bomber with more missions than this was 103 Sqn's Lancaster III ED888 *Mike Squared*, with 140.

Two days later *Sugar* flew to Brussels to repatriate Allied prisoners of war. It returned in the afternoon with around twenty former POWs, who were landed at Westcott, Buckinghamshire, before the bomber flew back to Waddington. *Sugar* was one of the first aircraft to undertake such a mercy flight. In all, 467 Sqn made twenty-seven such trips as part of Operation Exodus, of which a number involved *Sugar*.

On 7 May the squadron CO took *Sugar* on a tour of German cities to observe the effects of the

Opposite: Wearing its famous NO ENEMY PLANE WILL FLY OVER THE REICH TERRITORY quotation, S-*Sugar* is seen being prepared for its next sortie while marked up with ninety-eight bombs on its ops tally.
(IX Squadron Archives)

bombing raids and check the suitability of some German airfields for accepting heavy Allied aircraft. The 6 hour 45 minute trip included Mannheim, Kitzingen, Wurzburg and Frankfurt with *Sugar* reportedly becoming the first Lancaster to land on an 'enemy' airfield.

On 14 July 1945 Air Cdre T. Fawdry, Bomber Command Administration, wrote a letter to the Air Historical Branch reporting that R5868 was surplus to requirements, but due to its record number of sorties enquired whether any special disposal arrangements were needed for the aircraft; it was in very good condition and was therefore suitable for carrying out exhibition flights if necessary. The AHB replied on 30 July requesting that the aircraft be retained in storage.

It was transferred from 467 Sqn to 15 Maintenance Unit, RAF Wroughton, Wiltshire, on 9 August as a museum piece, though for a while it remained at Waddington. On 23 August it went to the MU as an exhibition aircraft. Then, on 1 August 1947, *S-Sugar* was declared non-effective stock, and on 16 March 1956 it was struck off charge as an exhibition aircraft and transferred to the Historical Aircraft Collection of the Air Historical Branch, still at Wroughton, being joined there by other AHB aircraft during that year.

During 1958 the bomber was moved to the AHB store at RAF Fulbeck, Lincolnshire, and was stored dismantled. In April 1959 the Lanc went back to its first base at RAF Scampton.

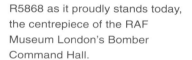

R5868 as it proudly stands today, the centrepiece of the RAF Museum London's Bomber Command Hall.

The originality of *S-Sugar*'s instrument panel conjures up thoughts of its crew climbing in and starting it up for another op.

It is thought-provoking to consider the view of the war that anyone might have had from the bomb aimer's position of this old warhorse.

The principal radio equipment in *S-Sugar*. The unit at the bottom right is the R.1155 receiver. The larger unit with coloured dials on top of the receiver is the T.1154 transmitter. To the left is the 'Fishpond' indicator, used to detect attacking enemy fighters.

The navigator's H2S equipment, with the indicator to the left and the switch unit to the right. Introduced in early 1942, H2S provided Bomber Command with ground-search mapping capabilities.

On 14 May 1959 it was displayed at a presentation by the Queen Mother of a standard commemorating the outstanding service of 617 Sqn to the unit. The aircraft was hangared on this occasion, still wearing its wartime colours and PO-S code. In 1960 it was placed on display at the station's main gate wearing 467 Sqn markings. In October 1960, 83 Sqn returned to Scampton, by then equipped with Avro Vulcans; when it was realised that *Sugar* had such strong links with the station and unit, the 467 Sqn codes were replaced by the original 83 Sqn OL-Q lettering. Of note, during its time on the gate at Scampton, certain components were removed for use in the restoration of PA474.

On 7 July 1970 R5868 was surveyed on site by a representative from 71 MU, Bicester, Oxfordshire, accompanied by Jack Bruce, Deputy Keeper of the RAF Museum. An external survey estimated that it would take 2,000 man-hours to cosmetically restore the aircraft for display. So on 26 August it was allotted to the RAF Museum at Hendon.

In November 1970 it was dismantled at Scampton by 71 MU and moved to Bicester for refurbishment. On 12 March 1972 the bomber was moved to Hendon by road in six Queen Mary loads, with an overnight stop at Northolt. Erection at Hendon was completed on 25 March. R5868 was then repainted at Hendon by a team from RAF St Athan, Wales. It was finished in the identity of *S-Sugar* of 467 Sqn, as it had been at the end of the war, and placed on view in the main aircraft hall when the museum opened. In August 1982 the Lancaster moved into the newly constructed Bomber Command Hall, where it still takes pride of place.

APPENDIX
Lancaster Survivors

L isted here are the seventeen Lancasters which remain as more or less complete airframes. Various cockpit sections (originals and mock-ups) also remain, but the only one listed in addition to the complete airframes is the IWM's Mk.I DV372 *Old Fred*, due to the fact that this Lanc served alongside *S-Sugar* and has been on display since just after the end of the Second World War. Brief directions and opening times are listed for all the UK sites, though not all the overseas locations have been treated so. Website details are, however, listed for all the Lancasters or their respective museums.

Mk.I R5868
RAF Museum London, Hendon, UK
Flagship of the RAF Museum London's Bomber Command Hall, R5868 *S-Sugar* is the oldest surviving Lancaster. The RAF Museum London is located on Grahame Park Way, Hendon, only six miles from central London, and is signposted from the end of the M1 motorway. Admission is free and the museum is open seven days a week except for Christmas and New Year. Tel: 0208 205 2266. **www.rafmuseum.org.uk**

Mk.I W4783
Australian War Memorial, Canberra, ACT, Australia
G-for-George now forms the centrepiece of the AWM's superb 'Striking by Night' audio-visual display. The AWM, on Treloar Crescent at the top of Anzac Parade in Canberra, Australian Capital Territory, is free to enter. It is open from 10 a.m. to 5 p.m. daily (9 a.m. to 5 p.m. during NSW/ACT school holidays). Closed on Christmas Day. **www.awm.gov.au**

The nose section of DV372 *Old Fred* on display at IWM London.
(Duncan Cubitt)

Mk.I DV372
Imperial War Museum London, Lambeth Road, London, UK

At the IWM London can be seen the nose section of Mk.I DV372 *Old Fred*, a former 467 Sqn Lancaster which flew alongside *S-Sugar* as PO-F between 5 November 1943 and 12 June 1944. It was put on display at the Lambeth Road museum from 19 November 1946, having been delivered there in June 1946 following its donation by the Air Ministry. The museum is free to enter. It is located on the A3203 east of Lambeth Palace and is well signposted. Tel: 020 7416 5320.
http://london.iwm.org.uk

Mk.X FM104
Toronto Aerospace Museum, Ontario, Canada

After spending thirty-four years outdoors on a plinth at Toronto's Harbourfront area, FM104 is now under restoration by the Toronto Aerospace Museum. The work is being carried out in a hangar that served as de Havilland Canada's Mosquito paint shop from 1943 to 1945. This Lancaster saw operational service with 428 Sqn during the Second World War, and postwar was converted into a Lancaster 10MR, serving on 107 Rescue Unit as CX-104. It was retired in 1962. **www.torontoaerospacemuseum.com**

Mk.X FM136
Aerospace Museum, Calgary, Alberta, Canada

Built by Victory Motors at Malton, Ontario, in late 1944, FM136 saw service with 404 'Buffalo' Sqn and 407 'Demon' Sqn, and was retired on 10 April 1961. The following year, it arrived at Calgary for external display on a plinth at the Centennial Planetarium, where it stayed for the next three decades or so. Once down from its plinth, it was taken on charge by the museum, which has fully restored its interior. Attention then turned to the exterior. **www.asmac.ab.ca**

Mk.X FM159
Nanton Lancaster Society and Air Museum, Nanton, Alberta, Canada

The centrepiece at this museum is FM159, which, although it saw no active service during the war, did serve later with the RCAF as a Lancaster 10MP. Retired in 1958, it was purchased by three enthusiasts in 1960 and put on display on the outskirts of Nanton. It suffered from vandals and souvenir hunters though, and by 1962 had been reduced to a shell. However, a group of volunteers embarked upon remedial work soon afterwards; during the mid-1980s NLS was formed, and a purpose-built hangar was provided for the Lanc in 1991. FM159's restoration has since continued apace, with the aim being to have the bomber's engines operational for ground-running; FM159 should be the next Living Lancaster! The first engine to come on line was No. 3, which was first fired up on 20 July 2005. **www.lancastermuseum.ca**

This is FM104 photographed in June 1998 while it was still mounted on its plinth on Toronto Harbourfront. It has since been taken down and is undergoing restoration at the Toronto Aerospace Museum.
(Duncan Cubitt)

Left: FM212 seen on 16 June 2004 in its former 'flying' configuration as it was displayed in the rose gardens in Jackson Park, Windsor, from 1965. Although painted in a camouflage bomber scheme, the Lancaster remains in its postwar RCAF configuration and as such has no gun turrets.

Below: Engine warm-ups ready for the last formation flight of the three remaining Lancaster 10ARs at RCAF Rockliffe, Ottawa, Ontario, on 14 January 1964. Most prominent in the picture is KB839, which is displayed at Greenwood, Nova Scotia. The picture is taken from on board KB976, which survives disassembled at Fantasy of Flight in Florida. Just visible behind KB839 are the tail fins of the third Lanc, KB882.
(Wouter van Warmelo)

Mk.X FM212
Windsor, Ontario, Canada

FM212 was the first Canadian-built Lancaster to be converted for photomapping purposes and was thus the prototype Mk.10P. It is now the only surviving Mk.10P, having been retired in 1962 after amassing a total of 8,069.5 hours' flying time. After retirement from the RCAF, in 1964 FM212 was moved to Windsor, going on display mounted on a plinth in Jackson Gardens the following year. Maintained by the Canadian Historical Aircraft Association, it serves as a memorial to the 400 local airmen who died in the Second World War, and wears the EQ-W code of a 408 'Goose' Sqn Lancaster. On 26 May 2005, having 'flown' on its plinth for forty years, FM212 was taken down and placed under cover.

The plan is eventually to house the Lanc inside a purpose-built museum facility at Windsor Airport, where it will be properly restored for long-term preservation.
www.lancasterfm212.freeservers.com

Mk.X FM213 (C-GVRA)
Canadian Warplane Heritage Museum, Hamilton, Ontario, Canada

Flying in the colours and markings of KB726 in honour of Plt Off Andrew Mynarski VC, FM213 is one of the world's only two airworthy Lancasters. It is maintained and operated by the CWHM. The museum is open year-round from 9.00 a.m. to 5.00 p.m., closed only on Christmas Day and New Year's Day. **www.warplane.com**

Mk.X KB839
Greenwood Military Aviation Museum, Nova Scotia, Canada

Built by Victory Aircraft at Malton, Ontario, KB839 served with 419 'Moose' Sqn RCAF, and

postwar was refurbished into Mk.10AR configuration. Earmarked for preservation, it moved to the military base at Greenwood for display in 1965. Still with the collection, in 2003 it underwent extensive conservation work, which included a repaint, and is now on show in the Aero Park as AF-A. **http://gmam.ca**

Mk.X KB882
St Jacques Airport, Edmundston, New Brunswick, Canada

KB882 flew to England in the spring of 1945 and saw operational wartime service with 428 'Ghost' Sqn. Postwar, it was converted to Mk.10AR standard and issued to 408 'Goose' Sqn based at RCAF Rockliffe, Ottawa, Ontario. After serving with the RCAF for almost twenty years, KB882 was struck off charge on 26 May 1964. It was flown to its current location for display on 14 July 1964 and is preserved in the silver and white livery of Air Transport Command. During the spring of 2005 meetings took place to consider the long-term future of this aircraft, which may see the Lanc eventually moved inside.
www.lancaster-kb882.freeservers.com/index.html

Mk.X KB889
Imperial War Museum Duxford, Cambridgeshire, UK

Manufactured by Victory Aircraft in Canada in late 1944, KB889 made the transatlantic flight to England in January 1945 and that April joined 428 'Ghost' Sqn. Postwar, KB889 was converted to Mk.10MP configuration, and following retirement from the RCAF moved in 1965 to the Niagara Falls-based Age of Flight Museum before being sold to a private collector some three years later. Acquired by Doug Arnold's Warbirds of Great Britain in 1984, KB889 gained the civil registration G-LANC, and it seemed that a return to the air was forthcoming. However, this was

KB882 during the final formation flight by the RCAF's last three Lancaster 10ARs from RCAF Rockliffe on 14 January 1964. This Lanc is now preserved at St Jacques, New Brunswick. (Wouter van Warmelo)

not to be, and with the help of the National Heritage Memorial Fund the Lancaster was passed on to the Imperial War Museum. It arrived at Duxford on 14 May 1986 and has since been fully restored wearing its accurate 428 Sqn code NA-I. It was officially unveiled on 1 November 1994. KB889 is one of more than thirty airframes earmarked to go on display in Duxford's new £24.7 million 'AirSpace' development, which will showcase British and Commonwealth aviation heritage and is scheduled to be opened in 2006. Duxford is located adjacent to the M11 at Junction 10, just south of Cambridge. The museum is open daily from 10 a.m. to 6 p.m. March to October, and 10 a.m. to 4 p.m. for the rest of the year. It is closed from 24 to 26 December. There is an admission fee for adults, although children under 16 are free. Tel: 01223 835000. **www.iwm.org.uk/duxford**

Mk.X KB944
Canada Aviation Museum, Ottawa, Ontario, Canada

This Lancaster joined the museum on 11 May 1964, after spending much of its service life in storage. Extremely well looked-after during its time with the museum, it is displayed as NA-P of 428 'Ghost' Sqn RCAF. KB944 is scheduled to

KB889 was formerly on display inside IWM Duxford's 'Superhangar', before the well-known structure began its redevelopment into the ambitious 'AirSpace' project. The Lancaster X is seen being moved outside to make a rare appearance in the daylight.
(Duncan Cubitt)

receive the markings it had in 1945 when it flew with 425 'Alouette' Sqn. Work began when the Lanc was moved into the new storage wing, which was completed during the summer of 2004. **www.aviation.technomuses.ca**

Mk.X KB976
Fantasy of Flight, Polk City, Florida, USA

This Lancaster was one of three heavily converted after the Second World War for use by the Canadian Forces in the Arctic Reconnaissance role. After retiring from military service, it was converted into a water bomber and put on the Canadian civil register as CF-TQC. It later joined the Strathallan Collection and flew to the UK for a rebuild to permanent flying condition as G-BCOH, by which time it was with Charles Church. Disaster struck on 12 August 1987, when the roof of its hangar at Woodford fell in and badly damaged the airframe. Since that time, the bulk of the project has moved across the Atlantic for storage at Kermit Weeks's Fantasy of Flight Museum, and parts from other Lancaster projects and Avro Lincoln components are believed to have been gathered for restoring it. While most of the parts are stored in containers, some items such as the centre section and outer wings have been placed elsewhere on site and were visible during the museum's 'Back Lot Tours'. Some sections of the aircraft may also still remain in the UK. **www.fantasyofflight.com**

Mk.VII NX611
Lincolnshire Aviation Heritage Centre, East Kirkby, Lincolnshire, UK

The pride of the Lincolnshire Aviation Heritage Centre, NX611 is a marvellous example of its type and much to the credit of all involved remains in taxiable condition. What's more, you can pay to experience a taxi ride in the Lanc!

Anyone wanting to book a place for a taxi run on board *Just Jane* should call Robert Gibson-Bevan on 01673 858387.

The museum can be found on the A155 west of Spilsby. Opening times from Easter to October are Monday to Saturday, 10 a.m. to 5 p.m. From November to Easter it is open from Monday to Saturday, 10 a.m. to 4 p.m. Please note that the LAHC is *not* open on Sundays. Taxi runs take place on various dates and are listed on the LAHC's website and in regular advertisements in the aviation press. Tel: 01790 763207. **www.lincsaviation.co.uk**

Mk.VII NX622
RAAF Association Aviation Heritage Museum, Bull Creek, Perth, Western Australia

Originally constructed for the RAF, this particular Lanc was one of the fifty-four supplied to France for use by the Aéronavale (Navy), who gave it the serial number WU-16. Upon retirement, this machine was presented to the Royal Australian Air Force Association (Western Australian Division) and flown to Perth. Repainted in RAF camouflage, it is now on display at Bull Creek. **www.raafawa.org.au/wa/museum/default.htm**

Mk.VII NX665
Museum of Transport and Technology, Austin, Auckland, New Zealand

New Zealand's only complete Lancaster is another former Aéronavale aircraft, having originally served as WU-13. Donated as a gesture of goodwill, it arrived at Austin on 15 April 1964 and has been comprehensively restored. Today, it is on show in the markings of PB457 of 101 Sqn on the port side and those of 75 (New Zealand) Sqn's ND752 on the starboard. **www.motat.org.nz**

Mk.I PA474
Battle of Britain Memorial Flight, RAF Coningsby, Lincolnshire, UK

Famous all over the world, BBMF's airworthy Lanc has been an integral part of the Flight ever since joining. Members of the public can be taken on guided tours into the BBMF hangar via the Battle of Britain Memorial Flight Visitor Centre at RAF Coningsby. Car parking is free, as is entry to the souvenir shop and exhibition area, but there is a small charge for guided tours of the hangar. With the exception of public holidays and two weeks over Christmas, the aircraft can be viewed every weekday from 10 a.m. until 5 p.m. The last guided tour begins at 3.30 p.m. If you are going especially to see the Lancaster, remember that during the flying season it is occasionally away. Call the visitor centre on 01526 344041 for further information, details of any special events or occasional weekend openings. Coningsby is located on the A153 south of Horncastle, from which follow the brown signs for the Battle of Britain Memorial Flight. **www.bbmf.co.uk**

For membership of Lincolnshire's Lancaster Association, please send a stamped addressed envelope to: Membership Secretary, Lincolnshire's Lancaster Association, PO Box 474, Lincoln, LN5 9ES. **www.pa474.f9.co.uk**

Mk.VII WU-21
Le Bourget, Paris, France

A highlight of the biennial Paris Air Show for many enthusiasts is the opportunity to see the ongoing progress with Lancaster VII NX664, which is undergoing comprehensive restoration at Le Bourget. The work is being undertaken by volunteers from Ailes Anciennes-Le Bourget, and is progressing extremely well. NX664 was built at Longbridge, Birmingham, in 1945 – just too late to see wartime service. After a period in storage, it became WU-21 with the French Navy in August

WU-16 while in service with the Aéronavale. NX622 is now at the RAAF Association Aviation Heritage Museum at Bull Creek in Australia. *(Ken Ellis Collection)*

At the Paris Air Show 2003, WU-21's nose section was displayed with a beautifully restored Merlin 24 alongside it.

1952 and was used for a variety of maritime tasks. On 26 January 1963, it was damaged in a landing accident at Wallis Island in the South Pacific and was written off – deemed not worth recovering. Nearly twenty-two years later, members of Ailes Anciennes mounted an epic rescue mission and brought WU-21 back to France for restoration. This was an enormous challenge, both in logistics and paperwork! By early 1986,

the Lancaster had arrived at its new home. Unfortunately, it was little more than a damaged empty shell. Since that time, the volunteers have worked wonders, with almost every area receiving attention – and regular appearances at the Paris show keep the superb project in the public eye. By the 2003 air show a group member had completed the painstaking restoration of one of the Merlin 24s, with work on its bearers having been started in 2002. All the other engine-bearer sets are badly corroded and will need to be fabricated. Most of the restoration inside the nose section has been completed, and a newly built electrical main distribution panel has now been fitted in the wireless operator's station. This had to be made from scratch, using as a guide a battered example recovered from a crash site and pictures from preserved aircraft. Attention has now turned to the fuselage centre section.

http://p51d20na.club.fr/wu21/lancasteracl_e.html

Bibliography

Bowyer, C., *For Valour – The Air VCs*, William Kimber, 1978

Falconer, J., *The Dam Busters*, Sutton, 2003

Flower, S., *A Hell of a Bomb*, Tempus, 2002

Gibson, G., *Enemy Coast Ahead – Uncensored*, Crécy, 2003

Goulding, B., Garbett, M. and Partridge J., *Story of a Lanc*,
   Lincolnshire Aviation Heritage Centre, 1974

Holmes, H., *Avro Lancaster – The Definitive Record*, Airlife, 1997

Lancaster, a *FlyPast* special publication, 1998

Leach, R.E., *A Lancaster At Peace*, Lincolnshire Lancaster Committee, 1981

Mason, F.K., *The British Bomber since 1914*, Putnam Aeronautical, 1994

Nelmes, M.V. and Jenkins, I., *G-for-George*, Banner, 2000

Page, B., *Mynarski's Lanc*, Boston Mills,
   1989

Sweetman, J., *The Dambusters
   Raid*, Arms and Armour, 1993

At many venues during the season, BBMF personnel freely distribute the relevant year's brochure. Watch out for one if you see them about, as these high-quality publications are most informative and very collectable.

Looking aft from the astrodome, as OC BBMF Sqn Ldr Clive Rowley MBE manoeuvres into position with Spitfire Vb AB910. *(Crown Copyright/MOD)*

A rare moment catching all three of the Lancaster's 2005 season captains together during pre-season training at Coningsby. From left to right: Sqn Ldr Stu Reid, Flt Lt Ed Straw and Flt Lt Mike Leckey.

Index